Praise for *Sacred Powers*

"Bright light, fully alive, wide awake, and overflowing with passion—these are just a few of the phrases I'd use to describe davidji. In *Sacred Powers*, you'll learn exactly what you need to do to emulate these beautiful qualities. You'd be hard-pressed to find a better guide for this life-changing, transformational journey!"

— Cheryl Richardson, *New York Times* best-selling
author of *Take Time for Your Life*

"When I read the first few pages of *Sacred Powers*, I was reminded of the very first time I encountered the joyful and brilliant davidji! It was a special moment for both of us—we felt an immediate soul connection and knew we would be collaborating for years to come. davidji has tapped into the secret of slipping into the stillness, where all things become crystal clear, and possibilities are limitless. *Sacred Powers* will resonate with anyone who finds themselves occasionally overwhelmed by daily challenges, with the nagging certainty that there 'must be something more.'"

— James Van Praagh, *New York Times* best-selling author of *Wisdom from Your Spirit Guides: A Handbook to Contact Your Soul's Greatest Teachers*

"*Sacred Powers* is essential reading for any serious seeker on the path of transformation. davidji is one of my favorite human beings on the planet, and has my deepest respect as a truly authentic and brilliant guide and teacher. This clear, intelligent, and exquisitely written book will serve as your new, delightful, and wise companion on the journey toward awakening."

— Dr. Barbara De Angelis, #1 *New York Times* best-selling
author of *Soul Shifts* and *The Choice for Love*

"While our experiences are all subjective and totally unique, there's always a truth concerning the objective framework of how and why our lives go the way they do. Enter my friend davidji, a wayfinder and mystic who has a most extraordinary grip on the truths that transcend both the objective and subjective worlds. His depth of experiences and tenacity of spirit have made him one of the pioneers of our time into all things body, mind, and spirit. As you feel his energy through his words, you too will know you've found a friend."

— Mike Dooley, *New York Times* best-selling
author of *Infinite Possibilities* and *Leveraging the Universe*

"Get ready to live the life you were meant to be living! davidji's personal transformation is a story that will have you tearing through this book at record speed, but it's the tools for personal transformation that will make you want to slow down and reexperience it over and over again. This is the real deal, filled with ancient wisdom modernized and directional moves to help you reach elevated states of consciousness and your full potential. *Sacred Powers* will amplify your heart, energy, and destiny."

— Suze Yalof Schwartz, founder and CEO of *Unplug Meditation*

"davidji threads pearls of wisdom through every page of *Sacred Powers*. He is a master storyteller, a beautiful wordsmith, who draws on a lifetime of spiritual adventures to help you say yes to your spiritual journey."

— Robert Holden, author of *Happiness Now!* and *Shift Happens!*

SACRED
POWERS

ALSO BY DAVIDJI

Books

destressifying: The Real World Guide to Personal Empowerment, Lasting Fulfillment, and Peace of Mind

Secrets of Meditation: A Practical Guide to Inner Peace and Personal Transformation

Video Training Courses

The Art of Meditation with davidji

Hay House University's 5-Week Meditation Program

Lightseeker: The Path to Spiritual Awakening

The Keys to Mindful Performance: Corporate Wellness Training

How Do I Know What I'm Supposed to Do?

Making the Big Decisions in Life

Meditated & Liberated with Libby C

Audio CDs and Digital Downloads

davidji Guided Meditations: Fill What Is Empty; Empty What Is Full: featuring Snatam Kaur and Damien Rose

40 Days of Transformation

Journey to Infinity: Music, Mantras, and Meditations with SacredFire Music

The davidji Meditation Experience—Volume 1

The davidji Meditation Experience—Volume 2

The Goddess Meditations, featuring Fionnuala Gill

Guided Meditations for Awakening Your Divine Self

davidji: Come Fly With Me

The Passenger's Guide to Stress-Free Flying

The Five Secrets of the SweetSpot: Rituals for Daily Meditation

davidji Guided Affirmations: Fill What Is Empty; Empty What Is Full

davidji Guided Meditations: Fill Your Chakras

Inspired by the Tulku Jewels Sacred Chakra Collection

davidji Guided Affirmations: Conscious Choices in Life and Love

***

SACRED POWERS

The Five Secrets to Awakening Transformation

 davidji

HAY
HOUSE

HAY HOUSE, INC.
Carlsbad, California • New York City
London • Sydney • New Delhi

Copyright © 2017 by davidji

Published in the United States by: Hay House, Inc.: www.hayhouse.com®
Published in Australia by: Hay House Australia Pty. Ltd.: www.hayhouse.com.au
Published in the United Kingdom by: Hay House UK, Ltd.: www.hayhouse.co.uk
Published in India by: Hay House Publishers India: www.hayhouse.co.in

The author gratefully acknowledges and credits Stephen Mitchell for his translation of the Tao Te Ching copyright (c) 1988 by Stephen Mitchell. Used by permission of HarperCollins Publishers.

Cover design: Amy Grigoriou • *Interior design: Karim J. Garcia*
Interior illustration: Courtesy of the author

Library of Congress Cataloging-in-Publication Data

Names: Ji, David, author.
Title: Sacred powers : the five secrets to awakening transformation / David Ji.
Description: 1st Edition. | Carlsbad : Hay House, Inc., 2017.
Identifiers: LCCN 2017033497 | ISBN 9781401952839 (tradepaper : alk. paper)
Subjects: LCSH: Spiritual life. | Spiritual formation. | Spirituality. | Awareness--Religious aspects.
Classification: LCC BL624 .J5 2017 | DDC 204/.4--dc23 LC record available at https://lccn.loc.gov/2017033497

Tradepaper ISBN: 978-1-4019-5283-9

16 15 14 13 12 11 10 9 8 7
1st edition, December 2017

Printed in the United States of America

A Native American folktale speaks eloquently to awakening
your Sacred Powers of Transformation.
A Cherokee elder is sitting around a bonfire with his grandchild,
teaching him the essentials of life.

"There is a battle going on inside me," he says to the child.
"It is a constant fight, and it is between two wolves.
One wolf is filled with anger, envy, jealousy, fear, regret, shame,
greed, arrogance, self-pity, guilt, resentment, inferiority,
false pride, superiority, and ego.

"The other wolf is filled with humility, gratitude, acceptance, patience, joy,
peace, love, hope, kindness, empathy, generosity, truth, and compassion."
He leans in close to his grandchild and whispers,
"The same fight is going on inside you, my sweet boy—
and inside every other person too."

The child grows silent, thinking about
the profound nature of this lesson,
and then asks,
"So, Grandfather . . . which wolf will win?"
The old Cherokee smiles with a knowing look and replies,
"The one you feed."

~ ~ ~

This book is dedicated to anyone who has ever asked,
"Which wolf will win?"

Life is a moving, breathing thing.
We have to be willing to constantly evolve.
Perfection is constant transformation.

— Nia Peeples

CONTENTS

PREFACE

The Moment of Your Awakening

If you're reading these words, you've already begun your journey on the spiritual path, or perhaps you're finding yourself at the crossroads of some potentially defining moment in your life. Maybe you're sensing a feeling of longing for something beyond what exists right now. Or you have confusion about the situation in which you currently find yourself. There may even be an indescribable sensation inside you—a sort of knowing that there's something more, something deeper, something better . . . a place where you can finally experience true love, real abundance, greater fulfillment, or simply peace of mind in the midst of all the chaos that surrounds you. Oftentimes we simply feel trapped by our current circumstances or locked into a non-nourishing pattern.

But there is a doorway to the liberation you now seek. In fact, there are five doorways and five paths that you can walk as you gain your footing on your spiritual journey. These paths are available to all seekers whether this is your first step into spirituality or whether you have been practicing for many years.

What has happened in the past can't be changed.
We can't unring the bell, but we can move forward . . .
and how you choose to move forward from this moment,
is the choice that will determine the fabric of your life.

Stepping through this doorway of spirituality will take you on a lifelong journey that will give you the power to make the most brilliant choice at the exact perfect time—one that will align you completely with the Universe; take your life to the next level; and awaken the divine nature that rests at your very core. Yes, you have *Sacred Powers of Transformation* resting deep within. Not simply the power to change but to truly transform your life to a place of deep fulfillment. *Transformation is evolution.* And it validates the eternal truth that you are never stuck. *You* always *have the power to shift your life* from where you are *to where you'd like to be* and where you truly *need to be.*

THE FIVE PATHS OF THE SPIRITUAL JOURNEY

The divine principles of the Universe will never change. They predate the Bible, the Torah, the Tao, the Rig Veda, and all of mankind. They existed from the very beginning. And for 10,000 years, they were woven into every indigenous culture on the planet through *sacred teachings* whispered directly into the hearts of priests, shamans, wizards, medicine women, and healers who led their ancient societies. But you don't need to be a mystic, a clairvoyant, or a guru to understand these divine principles. They are invisibly woven into every aspect of your existence. You will awaken each one of them in your life as we journey together.

For thousands of years, spiritual seekers have unveiled the five divine secrets of personal transformation by navigating five life-affirming paths as they travel along their journey:

1. *The Divine Path of One*
2. *The Divine Path of Awareness*
3. *The Divine Path of REbirth*
4. *The Divine Path of Infinite Flow*
5. *The Divine Path of Inner Fire*

Each divine path offers its own unique doorway to a treasure trove of Sacred Powers that—once awakened—will help you move beyond whatever blocks your way, unfold transformation in all areas of your life, and cultivate your ability to manifest your dreams and desires. Journeying along the Divine Path of One awakens your *Sacred Powers of Presence, Your Ripple*, and *Spirit*. Walking the Divine Path of Awareness awakens your *Sacred Powers of Attention, Intention*, and *Action*. Traveling the Divine Path of REbirth awakens your *Sacred Powers of Acceptance, Release*, and *New Beginnings*. Stepping on to the Divine Path of Infinite Flow awakens your *Sacred Powers of Trust, Abundance*, and *Shakti*. And exploring the Divine Path of Inner Fire awakens the *Sacred Powers of Your Heart, Passion*, and *Purpose*.

As you navigate each Divine Path and learn its timeless secret, the guidance you receive will progressively build on the wisdom of the previous path, like spiritual building blocks. This way, by the time you have journeyed through all five paths, you will be living your life through the *Five Divine Principles* that uphold the Universe. Together you and I will venture onto each of these transformational paths to learn their divine secrets and awaken the Sacred Powers that have been resting at your core since the moment the Universe first breathed life into you. Each step you take will unfold eternal truths to guide you on a lifelong journey of clarity and connection, expansion and abundance, love and happiness, courage and confidence, and passion and purpose. You will awaken a better version of yourself as you let go of what no longer serves you, strengthen your resolve, lean in the direction of your dreams, learn to step into your power, connect with divine spirit, and live the life you were meant to live.

No equipment is necessary. You already have everything you need to attain this heightened state of self-actualization. You simply need to trust, read on, and surrender to the guidance that follows. I'll be right here with you as we take our steps along the Five Divine Paths, uncovering their magnificent secrets. And I will share with you the eternal wisdom of the Sacred Powers, offering real-world solutions to help you transcend your current fears, blockages, and constrictions. Together, we will manifest our dreams!

INTRODUCTION

Sacred Whispers

Be willing to take the first step, no matter how small it is. . . .
Absolute miracles will happen.

— Louise Hay

IF YOU CAN DREAM IT . . .

There are times in our life when we need to reset our course, reinvent ourselves, recalibrate our circumstances, and establish a new trajectory. These are the defining moments when we need to draw a line between everything that's ever happened and everything that ever will. All the words society currently uses to describe these moments don't really do them justice—fresh start, new beginning, second chance. They just don't tell the full story. Because in reality, we desire a total extraction from the scenario we've created—with all its consequences and aftereffects—and *the chance for a complete do-over*, a reentry into a new world where we are whole, pure, perfect, unstained, untainted, and unconditioned.

Sometimes we're not aware that the critical moment has arrived. We have resigned ourselves to the fact that we must live with the cards we've been dealt, and, subsequently, we are blind to the amazing opportunity resting right in front of our noses.

More often than not, we can taste and feel—with every fiber of our being—that the Universe has taken a deep breath in, allowed time and space to pause, announced a special yet fleeting opportunity, and given us the chance to leap into a new, more nourishing dream. The greatest pioneer of the animation industry, Walt Disney, is often credited with saying, "If you can dream it, you can do it." He demonstrated this not just by powerfully manifesting his own dreams but by also awakening the dreams that rest inside each of us. His vast legacy of movies, theme parks, and cartoons taught (and continue to teach) millions of children and their parents around the world that we are beings of transformation, capable of manifesting whatever we desire.

Many people see the concept of manifesting their dreams as a fantasy. A lifetime of conditioning holds them back from taking that bold, transformational step. Fear keeps them frozen, clinging desperately to the old dream, and the throbbing pain of past missteps locks them into a swirl of second-guessing. And so they find themselves with one foot firmly planted in the past and one dangling toe waiting to touch down in the fresh, fertile soil of the newly envisioned future.

Some people spend their entire lives just like that—holding themselves back, trapped in a prison of their own design, deferring their dreams, and accepting a dumbed-down version of their best selves.

I was one of those people until I discovered the Five Divine Secrets and their Sacred Powers of Transformation.

LIFE AT THE CROSSROADS

Sleepwalking through life, the weight on my chest so heavy I could barely breathe, and working an 18-hour day in a business that did not feed my soul, I was stressed out, burned out, unfulfilled, and empty. I was so far from the present moment and living eternally in the past, carrying a knot in my stomach so tight that it could only be washed away by a glass of Scotch at bedtime. I had accepted that this would be my life and resigned myself to the sad reality that one day, I would die, and the nightmare would be over.

But then, in the wake of 9/11, at the four-way intersection of hopelessness, deep sadness, confusion, and lack of purpose, I walked past a row of cardboard boxes that people were living in on a street in downtown Manhattan. It was there that I received the first *Sacred Whisper* of my life—an unexpected moment in which time stood still and the voice of the Divine spoke directly to me through the body of someone I did not know and had never met. This life-changing hiccup in the space-time continuum was a defining moment of celestial convergence that absorbed me into a cosmic stream of timelessness—and ultimately gave me a new-found awareness and the inspiration to dream a new dream.

At first I was startled as I glimpsed a soot-covered hand reaching out from a blanket-covered cardboard structure to grab my pant leg as I walked by. But instead of speeding up and brushing past, *for some reason*, I slowed down, stopped, leaned back on my left foot, and offered my right leg as if I were in a trance and had no choice. I watched the hand extend farther toward me, gripping a fold of my pant leg right beneath my knee. And suddenly the moment began revealing itself in slow motion. I gasped, and my throat closed tightly, holding my breath in for a second. Then it felt as though the heavens opened up—everything moved away from us—the sky distanced itself, the other people on the sidewalk vanished, the buildings around us evaporated. It was as if the two of us were the only creatures in existence. All the street sounds and voices around us faded into the background as a high-pitched *whoosh!* encased my head like the sound in your ears as you lay in bed after you've attended a really loud concert. And the grizzled face of a man, with dirt deeply etched into the crevices of his forehead and hollowed-out cheeks, peered up at me.

He tightened his grip, pulling my attention down with his fingers as he hoisted his body up and inched his face a bit closer to mine. We leaned into each other and matched gazes. Our eyes locked for what seemed an eternity. Those deep-aquamarine pools dazzled me, inviting me into the depths of his soul. And with a raspy whispered breath, he spoke as if forcing me to bear the burden of the words he uttered. His lips parted, and he asked, "What's going to be on your tombstone?"

THE DEFINING MOMENT

The words swept into my mind and echoed over and over. They cascaded down from my ears, past my throat to my shoulders, dripping down my chest, racing into my heart, each syllable integrating itself into every cell of my body, and then bursting back out of my solar plexus, until they puddled on the sidewalk between us. I remember gasping as our eyes stayed riveted on each other's pupils. And then he loosened his fingers and released his grip, his hand sliding down the front of my pant leg and resting on my shoe.

It was most likely seconds, but it felt like hours. Sensing his knuckles resting on my shoe with his open palm faceup, I assumed he was asking for some charity. I reached into my pocket, intending to give him a few dollars. Clairvoyantly, he reached up to stop me and pressed his hand against my pocket, pinning my hand inside it. "It's not about the money. The answer is in the stars," he counseled in a raspy whisper. "Just find your sacred powers."

Suddenly realizing that I had not breathed in a minute, I gasped again. And as I exhaled back out, all I could utter was, "Huh?" I backed up a few inches, freeing my hand from his pressure, and, as if on autopilot, plucked a few bills from my pocket in slow motion. Again, I took a long, slow, deep breath in and extended my hand to make an offering. He countered with a whisper and a gaze up to the heavens. "Can you hear it? Do you hear that?"

BREATHING IN THE DIVINE

There was total silence. The whooshing had stopped. No sounds of the city. No sounds of anything. The space between his words was deafening. It was a moment of pure quiet. My heart felt so peaceful. My mind was a serene pond. There was no movement within us or around us. We were merged. There was nothing. It was nothingness. Timelessness. One-ness.

As we remained frozen in this moment, without breaking his gaze or moving his lips, he said, "Now you see me. And now I see you. Will you trust?"

That's right. His lips were closed. But the words flowed out of him and came into me! Uncontrollably, my fingers opened and dropped the bills on the concrete in front of his box. I stared at him deeply and took another long, slow, deep breath as if I were inhaling his very essence—his words, his sparkling blue eyes, his pain, his heart, his grime, his love, his wisdom, his rapture became mine. And for the first time in decades, I felt so light, so free, so awake and knowing, weightless, pure, whole, loved, and filled with clarity. Everything made sense. I can only describe it as a feeling of total completeness. I wanted to absorb the moment forever. But awareness of time and space began to creep back into the bliss, and I felt the sensation of slowly moving back into my physical body. Then there were the sounds of the city again—car horns, traffic, footsteps, people's voices. Suddenly staring at him became too uncomfortable—then it became painful. I broke our gaze, looked away, and became aware of my setting. The bills lay on the concrete separating us.

I bent down to pick them up and hand them to him, but he had already withdrawn into the darkness of his cardboard room. I tucked the bills inside the curtain of blankets that acted as his doorway. I stood there waiting for him to reappear, but I never saw him again. I turned away and continued walking. But I had only traveled 20 feet before I felt the need to stop and rest.

My knees were weak, my heart was pounding—and I was having trouble catching my breath. Tears streamed from the corners of my eyes, and beads of sweat dripped down my forehead onto my trembling lips. My mind was racing as I tried to comprehend what had just occurred. My hands were shaking, and my feet became wobbly. So I sat down on a stone doorstep in front of an apartment building and replayed the experience over and over and over in my mind's eye. The man had spoken only a few sentences, but they were now deeply carved into my soul: *"What's going to be on your tombstone?" "It's not about the money." "The answer is in the stars." "Just find your sacred powers." "Can you hear it?" "Do you hear that?" "Now you see me." "And I see you." "Will you trust?"* I sat for an hour lost in thought as I integrated the encounter into every fiber of my being.

I could have chosen to ignore the whole experience. Even chalk it up to just another kooky interaction in crazy New York City. But it zapped me so deeply to my core, and I couldn't shake it. I actually felt it changing me cell by cell as it rippled through my consciousness.

SURRENDERING TO THE LIGHT OF TRANSFORMATION

I didn't know it then, but in that defining moment, my entire existence would be transformed forever. I felt the Universe open up and invite me in. My perception began to shift in ways I would only come to understand years later. And, for the life of me, I can't pretend to really even know what actually happened. Was this dear homeless man a messenger from the beyond? Had I just had a conversation with the Divine? Did I have a mini-breakdown? Had I hallucinated the entire experience? Within a few hours— my whole world started powerfully transforming.

By the next morning, all the hair on my head—red since my birth—began to lose its pigment and turn white. The world around me had taken on an entirely different look, and I felt as if a shroud had been lifted. There was a new, fresh *lightness* to each moment, an ease that rippled through me. My thoughts unfolded with laser clarity. My conditioned perspectives of life began to unravel, replaced with innocent eyes and a beginner's mind. Flickers of peacefulness began inserting themselves into every conversation, action, and experience. I slept deeply and restfully like I did when I was a kid. I awoke each morning filled with gratitude and enthusiasm—so excited to be alive. And by the weekend, love-filled light was pouring into my heart, replacing the dark decades of sadness and allowing me to experience joy for the first time in years. In the blink of an eye, I had been transformed.

Weeks later, after an 18-year career in the business world, I found myself trekking through the jungles of southern India, experiencing energetic awakenings that powerfully shifted my physical body, my worldview, and my ability to see beyond the current moment. And, as it turned out, my encounter on that crisp September morning was only the first of many more mystical awakenings that revealed themselves to me over the next decade.

Over the years, I've experienced similar inexplicable encounters, which have gifted me with profound insights, higher states of consciousness, and timeless wisdom to guide me into deeper levels of understanding about life, love, purpose, and decision making. In the deep recesses of my heart, I have referred to these experiences as *butterfly moments* because each has left me totally transformed from where I was only a few minutes before. I briefly mentioned this very first butterfly moment in my first book, *Secrets of Meditation*. But never before have I revealed the conversation that changed my life, the life lessons that followed, or how I learned to awaken the Sacred Powers that were shared with me as I continued journeying on the Divine Path.

THE POWER OF THE BUTTERFLY

On each of these occasions, the heavens part, time slows to a standstill, and I am surrounded by a bubble of silence. My focus zeros in on the other person, and I am aware only of their piercing eyes, which lock me in for what feels like eternity. And then someone I've never met delivers a profound message that has opened another doorway to my personal transformation.

Each time, these butterfly moments rock me for days, weeks, and months as I attempt to integrate their intensity, profundity, and meaning. Each defining moment has acted as a powerful path to deep, personal evolution. Sometimes they occur while I am at a major fork in the road. And other times they come out of the blue, revealing a magnificent crossroads to which I was oblivious up until that moment. But each time they have acted as the stepping-off point into timeless wisdom.

Almost immediately after my *"What's going to be on your tombstone?"* butterfly moment, I left my career, unplugged from my existence as I knew it, and began a lifelong devotional quest to understand what had actually occurred that day, to discover the Sacred Powers, and to learn the Five Eternal Secrets of Transformation.

A DATE WITH DESTINY

My *next* butterfly moment unfolded several months later as I was traveling through southern India after weeks of scouring the Himalayan foothills in the north for answers. There I had been told of a mystical shaman who could see deep into the past and far into the future of those who were destined to visit him. He was known as the *Nadi*, which means "palm leaf" in Tamil, a language of southern India that has been spoken for more than 2,000 years. I had spent many weeks traveling thousands of miles—from the north to the south—roaming from one village to the next in search of deep answers. I kept bumping into dead ends, and no one who even spoke my language, which made me question whether it was truly meant to be. But I persevered, because somewhere in my heart, I felt divinely directed to find him.

On this particular day, I sensed I was getting closer as I stood in a busy marketplace with my pink skin and white hair attracting a swarm of people who wanted to hug me and take photos with me. I spoke neither Tamil nor Hindi, and no one around seemed to speak English. And then *Boom!* As soon as I uttered the word *nadi*, everything went silent. The noise of the market stilled to a hush. I could feel the wings of the butterfly starting to emerge from its chrysalis. The crowd faded into the background as a slender teenage boy approached me and gazed deeply into my eyes. In total silence, we stared at each other for what seemed like an hour, though it was most likely a few minutes. He extended his hand, and I took it as he led me past the hundreds of swarming onlookers through a twisting maze of side streets and back alleys. Finally, we emerged at a curbside kiosk, where he ordered two cups of tea. As we stood in the dusty road, sipping from our glasses and staring into one another's eyes, I realized I was on the very edge of another powerful transformation.

We drank in silence, and then he ordered us another cup and began to speak to me in an unknown language. At first I just listened as his words penetrated my heart. But after a while, it morphed into a "conversation," as I began to tell him about my journey and how I was sensing that this was another butterfly moment. Our eyes were riveted, and although he only knew Tamil and clearly did not understand English, he acknowledged every word I spoke as if he fully comprehended it, nodding and smiling at me with his jet-black eyes.

STRANGER IN A STRANGE LAND

And so there we stood in the street, speaking *at* each other and never understanding a word the other was saying. But a sweet vibration seemed to be flowing between us, and we laughed a lot and started to cultivate a comfort. Using some made-up sign language, bizarre body language, and lots of repetition, over 20 minutes, I was able to learn that his name was Rakesh, and he'd heard of the Nadi but never actually seen him. An hour later, he was driving me from the market in his broken-down jalopy on a dirt road that supposedly would take me to meet the Nadi. He kept giggling, and I kept trusting. It was beyond weird, but how could I resist?

We traveled for six hours by car with him chattering nonstop in Tamil and me telling him about my *"What's going to be on your tombstone?"* butterfly moment. We stopped to fill the tank once, and he even giggled and chattered away as he pumped the gas. Even though neither of us had a clue of what the other was saying, it seemed we had become fast friends. We laughed, sang, and drank in the amazing scenery as we got farther and farther away from civilization. There were times where the road was so narrow that his car barely squeezed between trees that bordered it, but we traveled onward and deeper into the unknown. At one point, he jammed on the brakes and jumped from the car, pointing in the distance to a long, smooth gray mountain on the other side of a lake. "Elephant rock! Elephant rock!" he shouted, so filled with glee. And, indeed, the mountain was in the shape of a huge elephant lying on its belly—it must have been 500 feet long.

We drove farther, entering the jungle near a town called Swamimalai, where he stopped the car, turned to me, giggled, and whispered, "Sacred Powers." I stared at him in awe; he gazed back with delight.

TRUSTING THE SIGNS

Was this another sacred whisper or was he just repeating the only two English words he remembered from a story I had told him five hours earlier? To this day, I don't have a clue. But we left the car when the dirt road became an even narrower walking path, and he continued to chatter away as he led me on foot into a jungle. Yes. I know what you're thinking. Wandering into the jungle in Tamil Nadu, filled with tigers, crocodiles, wild boars, monkeys, and the occasional elephant, being escorted by some kid you've just met, who doesn't speak or understand your language, and probably doesn't even have a driver's license in a country 10,000 miles away from home might not be wise.

But I was on a mission. And if this guy was going to introduce me to one of the greatest oracles on the planet who could answer my questions, then I was going to take a shot and follow his lead. I had literally traveled to the other side of the world on the recommendation of the man in the cardboard box, who had asked me, "Will you trust?" My heart said to trust in the moment, so I surrendered and we kept hiking. As we walked through the winding jungle path, we both stopped talking and instead listened to our footsteps, the squawking of birds, and the rustling of leaves.

THE HANDOFF

After walking through the jungle in silence for an hour, we came upon a thatched-roof hut, where Rakesh presented me to a slight man in his 30s named Nannan, who spoke and understood both Tamil and English. They chatted for a while, and I kept hearing the word *nadi*, but I understood nothing else in their conversation. And then Rakesh pointed to Nannan, excitedly laughing the words, "Nadi! Nadi! Nadi!" Rakesh hugged me, pulling me close and whispering in my right ear, "Sacred Powers, Mr. David," smiling a huge grin that filled me with such happiness—so much joy, I can feel it right now—and perhaps you can too. Then he spun on his heel and began walking back on the path that had led us there. Within a few moments, he had vanished into the depths of the jungle.

Nannan smirked, rocked his head from side to side, and formally introduced himself to me with a firm handshake. "Are you the Nadi?" I asked. He laughed and in perfect English, with a heavy Indian accent, he said, "No. I am simply Nannan. But I know where the Nadi lives. And tomorrow I will take you to him and translate for you." I asked if Rakesh would be okay wandering back through the jungle, and Nannan assured me he'd navigate his way back to the car with no difficulty. Then he showed me to a pile of blankets on my side of the hut, where I'd be sleeping that night. He poured me some tea, and we sat on the dirt floor and chatted for a few hours until the sun set.

I shared with him my amazement at how everything had unfolded for me over the past several months. He was unfazed. Apparently, he had brought many people to the Nadi over the years. He calmly told me, "There are no meaningless coincidences, Mr. David. If you are meant to see the Nadi, this is how it happens." Then we shared some bean stew that he had been cooking in a pot on a bonfire in front of the hut. He tended the fire for a while to keep away the animals, and then we sat silently in the darkness, listening to the crackling of the embers and the amazing night sounds of the jungle. Before long, I was asleep.

SOUL JOURNEY

When I awoke the next morning, we meditated together on the jungle floor with nature surrounding us. As we began our trek to meet the Nadi, I asked him what his name meant. He proudly beamed. "*Nannan* means 'brave man.'" He flexed his biceps for emphasis. We traveled the rest of the way in silence, and my mind was awash—replaying all that had transpired the day before and the experience now unfolding.

Hours later, I was sitting in a room with Nannan and the Nadi, a very serious shaman, who spoke only in deep, grunting whispers and only in the language of ancient Tamil. Every word between me and the Nadi needed to pass through Nannan, and I suddenly had a deep wave of gratitude for Rakesh, who had so kindly taken care of me, delivering me to this auspicious moment. The Nadi held up his hand and pointed to his right thumb. I offered him mine and he swabbed it in a black liquid. Then he pressed it down for a few seconds on a piece of paper and left the room with my thumbprint.

Nannan and I sat in silence for a long time, as the Nadi meditated in another room. When he came back, he asked me a series of yes/no questions about my life and left the room again. When he returned, he had retrieved an ancient browned parchment made of the dried leaf of a Palmyra palm tree, and he placed it on the table between us. "This is your leaf," Nannan informed me. "The story of your soul's entire existence." The strange, stiff, dark-golden leaf was inscribed with tiny etchings in black ink, which had been made hundreds of years earlier from a mixture of the dried lamp soot of sesame oil, rainwater, and the gum of an acacia plant. The etchings were in ancient Tamil, composed of an alphabet totally unknown to me, and mysterious symbols that resembled Egyptian hieroglyphics.

The palm leaf reader started deciphering the document, and began whispering its contents in the language of ancient Tamil. And for 10 continuous hours, as the Nadi relentlessly read aloud, Nannan translated these whispers into English, sharing with me the wisdom of the cosmos, revealing all the details of my past lives, my future lives, and every aspect of my current life—including the moment of my death. He revealed secrets I had never shared with anyone—defining moments from my childhood, ailments, surgeries, major life decisions I had made that set me on certain paths, even confidences regarding my parents, workmates, and lovers. Every so often, when details from my past came out into the open, I would confirm them, and respond, "Wow! You're really good, Nadi." But he was unwilling to take the credit for being clairvoyant. Each time, Nannan would reply, "He says he's simply reading the leaf." And yet he discussed my life in such faceted nuance that I was left awestruck in every moment.

DEEPER INTO THE LEAF

Hour after mind-blowing hour, we explored the sacrosanct and the mundane: from the eternal lessons of the Five Divine Principles, which have guided the heavens and the earth since time began, to the 18-year business career I had just left; my struggles and challenges with life and love, and the choices I had made to bring me to this auspicious place in my transformation; he clarified my divine purpose here on earth; and explained to me in detail the enduring wisdom and transformational abilities of each of the Sacred Powers.

We explored how I had died in several of my past lives and why I kept coming back to clear my karma. He picked apart every decision I had ever made in this life and how they had led me to this most defining moment of my existence. He told me about families I had been part of, going back hundreds of years; colleagues I had worked with; partners I had supported; friends I had trusted; lovers I had intimately shared with; children I had fathered; people I had betrayed; hearts I had broken. No stone was left unturned.

Then he revealed how my life would unfold from that day forward, the choices that I'd make, right down to how I would die, and when. And through it all, I stared deeply into the Nadi's eyes, listening to the raw truth of my existence coming from Nannan's lips, as the Nadi continued grunting his *Sacred Whispers* in ancient Tamil. My pen took on a life of its own as I furiously scribbled down the details on nearly a hundred pages of my journal, stopping only when the Nadi had uttered his last whisper and Nannan said, "It is finished."

The three of us were exhausted, and we slid from our chairs onto the rug beneath us. I curled up in a fetal position and began to sob. I struggled to catch my breath as tears streamed down my cheeks into small pools on the worn-out carpet. The raw truth of the experience had cut so sharply into my heart that I continued to cry for days, as I literally integrated 10 lifetimes of information, knowledge, and wisdom into my being. I left the Nadi transformed forever, holding his *Sacred Whispers* deep inside my soul, and solemnly rededicated myself to living every breath with deeper meaning and purpose.

DIVINE GUIDANCE

Since that day, I have continued to study the foundations of this timeless body of knowledge with some of the greatest masters and healers of our time—exploring the most potent wisdom traditions of diverse cultures, practicing them with my students, testing ancient theories in real-life situations, and applying them to real-world challenges. I have embraced the Five Divine Principles as powerful ways to perceive and receive the world around me. These consciousness-based principles are the foundation of my core values; they guide my thoughts, decision making, and actions. I have carved them into every fiber of my being, and they act as nourishing guardrails as I navigate life's twists and turns.

And just as the Five Divine Principles guide my very essence, the Sacred Powers that flow from them flow through me with every breath. I awaken them each morning to begin my day with gratitude, passion, purpose, and an open heart. And I invoke them in my darkest hours, my moments of feeling stuck or indecisive, and in situations where I don't know how to proceed. Integrating these Sacred Powers allows me to effortlessly evolve chaos into calm, pain into joy, dreams into reality, and an empty heart into one that radiates deeper love and compassion.

Awakening the Sacred Powers every day has consistently guided me from uncertainty and change to a place of truth, clarity, courage, and strength. As I have journeyed to master these powers, I have shared aspects of them in my Teacher Trainings and spiritual healing workshops. *But time is precious, the clock is ticking, and I am being called right now to share with you the entire body of timeless knowledge that has been shared with me.* If you continue to journey further with me, I'll teach you how to transform darkness into light, the sublime into the practical, and the cosmic into the personal.

The Sacred Powers are as old as the heavens and have guided man and womankind toward powerful transformation as long as the stars have dotted the night sky. Yet so much of this wisdom has been forgotten in the swirl, speed, and complexity of our modern world, which has more moving parts, more people, and more scenarios than ever existed before.

So, if you are finding yourself at a crossroads, a fork in the road, a dead end, or a place of uncertainty, allow me and these teachings to be a soothing balm to your pain . . . a light of hope in your darkness . . . and a whisper of clarity and comfort to your heart as together we awaken your best version.

THE BLUEPRINT FOR TRANSFORMATION

In the following pages, you and I will explore the Five Divine Paths leading to the wisdom of the Five Divine Principles. Together we will step through the doorways that reveal their eternal, transformational, and life-affirming secrets. We will dive deep into the *Sacred Powers of Transformation*—timeless access points to awakening the life you've always dreamed—that are waiting for us on each path. As the essence of these principles and their powerful practices gently start to unfold with each thought you have, they will flow into your words, and then into your actions. Ultimately, the transformation will ripple through every fiber of *your* BEing— nourishing you, fueling you, inspiring you, and guiding you past fear to your best version. You'll be more prepared to take that step, make that move, own your decision, and step into your power.

If you are suffering any emotional pain right now, walls that you may have built around your heart will begin to soften as compassion and forgiveness start to replace your grudges and grievances. No longer will you feel separate from the Universal flow of life. Courage will replace fear, clarity will replace indecision, enthusiasm will replace excuses, and happiness will begin flowing to you effortlessly.

If you haven't ever read one of my books, watched my videos, or journeyed with me in person, allow me to explain a little bit about my style. I'm not a guru; I'm a translator. I've apprenticed under several great masters and studied the ancient texts for decades, but I find greater value in real-world practice rather than talking theory. When it comes to specific wisdom traditions or schools of philosophy, I honor all belief systems, but I am not big on rules. So I have woven my own spiritual tapestry made up of a multitude of threads from many bodies of knowledge, which I find to be more inclusive, more accessible, and more easily translated into practice.

If you are ready to continue with me, I've laid out our journey in a format that will allow you to effortlessly weave all this timeless wisdom into the fabric of *your* life. The teachings in Chapter 1, "The Energy of Transformation," are the platform for taking our first steps. You'll learn how the entire Universe flows through you and how you can harness that divine energy to manifest your dream life.

We'll then begin our expedition by stepping on to the first path of the spiritual journey and opening the door to the first eternal secret:

The Divine Principle of One

You'll learn how awakening the *Sacred Powers of Presence, Your Ripple*, and *Spirit* enlightens you to the sacred, precious present moment; flows your impact throughout the world; and merges your soul with the Divine Spirit.

Once you are established in this state of one-ness, we will step on to the second path of the spiritual journey, opening the door to the second eternal secret:

The Divine Principle of Awareness

We'll explore how awakening the *Sacred Powers of Attention, Intention*, and *Action* settles your thoughts and calms your mind; clarifies your intentions; and manifests your dreams and desires.

As you become more comfortable with the expansive power of your *true* awareness, we will begin walking the third path of the spiritual journey, where we will open the door to the third eternal secret:

The Divine Principle of REbirth

You'll learn how awakening the *Sacred Powers of Acceptance, Release,* and *New Beginnings* enables you to make peace with your past; let go of what no longer serves you; step into your power; and unapologetically own your impact.

Once you are no longer weighted down by a lifetime of baggage, we will take our first steps on the fourth path and open the door to the fourth eternal secret on the spiritual journey:

The Divine Principle of Infinite Flow

You'll discover how awakening the *Sacred Powers of Trust, Abundance,* and *Shakti* moves you past fear; opens your life to infinite possibilities; and accelerates your ability to easily channel the Universe.

With the Universe at your back, as trust is flowing through every fiber of your being, we will step on to the fifth path and open the door to the fifth eternal secret:

The Divine Principle of Inner Fire

You'll learn how activating the *Sacred Powers of Your Awakened Heart, Passion,* and *Purpose* fills each moment with unconditional love; stokes the fire of your deepest desires; and crystallizes the deeper meaning of your life.

How you see the world will change, and how the world sees you will shift. You will begin living a life of your own design, making bold, fearless choices and having them validated by the Universe. And with each day, as you become more familiar with the Five Divine Principles and their Sacred Powers, the inner whispers of your soul will naturally become your outer voice. You don't have to "try" or "do" anything . . . the transformation will be effortless. Simply understanding the Divine Principles and awakening each Sacred Power as part of who you are will transform the physical, emotional, material, relationship, and spiritual realms of your life.

CHAPTER ONE

THE ENERGY OF TRANSFORMATION

And men said that the blood of the stars flowed in her veins.

— C. S. Lewis

Universal principles have existed since time began. Gravity, electricity, temperature, light—they flow through the cosmos and every facet of existence. They are mostly invisible, as they work magically in the background of every moment. Whether we exactly understand the science behind how they function is not as critical as knowing these principles have overseen our galaxy from the very beginning.

The sun's electromagnetic power warms our bodies and the ground we walk upon, transforms the oceans into rain, fuels plant and animal life, and energizes the cycles of the seasons. The moon rhythmically spins around the earth as we swirl around the sun in a cosmic dance of celestial proportion. Light-filled glass bulbs of every shape and size adorn the planet, piercing the darkness in bedrooms, bridges, skyscrapers, and stadiums. We see, hear, touch, taste, smell, and feel these Universal codes of existence expressing themselves in every moment as the wonders of nature unfold around us and within us. And regardless of our culture, our belief system, our religion, or our ethnic background, these timeless principles of the Universe interweave like instruments in a cosmic symphony orchestra.

OUR TRUTH RESTS IN THE STARS

The eternal codes of nature embedded in the fabric of our existence have cradled our sweet Mother Earth for more than four billion years. And as human civilization took its first baby steps less than 10,000 years ago, ancient sages, scholars, and healers revealed the undeniable connections between these forces of nature and sacred transformational powers resting within human beings. Modern astronomy now confirms that the same ingredients that make up the galaxy are actually the same ones rippling through our bodies. We are stardust. Yes. I know it sounds very romantic, perhaps even kooky, but the truth is that almost everything on earth was created at the heart of a star.

We've all heard the term *supernova*. This is what happens to a star at the end of its life. It explodes. And the resulting nuclear blast releases all the elements that rest at its core—hydrogen, helium, oxygen, carbon, iron, nickel—all the stuff that makes up life on this planet and in our bodies. We don't need to be experts in the science of nebulae, nucleosynthesis, stellar theory, or gravity to grasp the concept that everything resting in the soul of the Universe is also resting at the center of life on earth and at the very center of our soul.

The exact same elements at the heart of a star flow through every plant, tree, ocean, mountain, bird, fish, animal, and human. You are stardust breathing stardust. Your heart is stardust beating stardust. Your eyes are stardust reading stardust. And your brain is stardust thinking stardust! Every moment is a stardust moment.

And just as the properties of physics, science, and mathematics seem to hold the stars apart, the planets in orbit, and our world from spinning out of control, *there is an even more powerful set of divine principles that exist within us* to hold our personal universe together. They are known as the *Five Divine Principles*—and each principle is built upon three *Sacred Powers of Transformation*.

Once we grasp these *Sacred Powers*, awaken them in ourselves, and realize their evolutionary impact on our life, we can use them in every moment to ground us, strengthen us, make better decisions, heal our relationships, and move us forward toward our best self.

THE HEARTBEAT OF THE UNIVERSE

"As is the cosmic body, so is the personal body; as is the cosmic mind, so is the personal mind."

This verse from The Puranas, an ancient Indian text believed to be thousands of years old, has also been translated as, "You are not *in* the Universe . . . the Universe is *within* you." The entirety of all existence rests at the very core of who you are.

That's right! Our original thread of life—when the DNA in our mother's egg merged with the DNA in our father's sperm— formed an entirely new organism with a master plan unique to you that was infused with the entire Universe resting within the tiniest of cells.

And in that moment, your stardust blueprint began repeating itself over and over and over again in a never-ending pattern that would become the platform for the transformation of your physical, emotional, and spiritual energy for the span of your lifetime.

This magnificent repeating pattern occurs throughout all aspects of life on earth. We see it most obviously in the crystalline structure of snowflakes that start with one droplet of water and replicate themselves over and over until they become the frozen geometrically perfect flake. The blueprint of a mighty oak tree stretching to the heavens lays curled up inside the tiniest of acorns. The symmetrical development of ferns, quartz geodes, nautilus shells, and heads of broccoli—even the beating of our hearts and the echoes of ocean waves—are larger-scale expressions of the very first cells that birthed them. Everything in nature is moving to the same primal beat—the heartbeat of the Universe.

ALIGNMENT IS EVERYTHING

Although we may not hear it in every moment, the subtle vibration and expansion of our stardust birth continuously plays through every cell of our existence, creating the soundtrack of our life. It weaves through our consciousness with every flicker of light, every breath someone takes, every thought that flows through our awareness, every conversation, and every interaction.

When we are fully aligned with the cosmic rhythm of all existence, our minds are clear; our eyes are bright; our words ripple from our lips with brilliance; our choice making is masterful; our actions are purposeful and compassionate; our hearts are peaceful, needing no defense or protective mechanism; grievances, grudges, and regret drift away; the impact of our interactions leaves sweetness and comfort with others. When we are fully aligned with the Universe, the energetic properties of the *Sacred Powers of Transformation* are deeply embedded within us, raising our vibration in every moment.

And just like keeping the beat with a song allows you to sing along with it, dance to it, hum it *even when it's not playing*, when you are aligned with the flow of the *Sacred Powers of Transformation*, you move your life to them, speak from their source, and dance to their cosmic rhythm.

Alignment is everything.

THE SOURCE OF *THE SACRED POWERS OF TRANSFORMATION*

For thousands of years, the great sages of the planet drew upon this vast body of cosmic knowledge—studying, practicing, and ultimately mastering these special Sacred Powers—using them to raise their own vibrations, elevate their consciousness, align with the Universal flow, and transform their lives. In time, under the guidance of these sages, seers, prophets, and masters, their early civilizations understood the celestial movements of the night sky, the cycles of the moon, our deep connection to the earth, air, and waters of the planet, and the interdependence of all living beings on this galactic grain of sand we call Earth.

But they were not simply scholars, scientists, astronomers, and mathematicians. They were also healers, mystics, and empaths, who understood the profound spiritual power and restorative impact of this primal life force in the minds and hearts of their tribes, clans, and communities. They were the true masters of the soul. And in their infinite wisdom, they taught their most devoted followers how to embrace the energy of the Universe, connect to its power, understand its impact, turn good intentions into great choices, make challenging decisions, move beyond constricting emotions, heal themselves, live with deeper meaning, experience freedom, and awaken grace in every moment.

Since my transformational session with the Nadi all those years ago, as my life has ebbed and flowed, I have woven this vast body of timeless wisdom through every aspect of my existence to help me find clarity, calm, compassion, insight, love, courage, inspiration, and fortitude. I've participated in tribal practices, prayer rituals, healing ceremonies, and out-of-body experiences, devoutly apprenticing under some of the great shamans, psychics, healers, rinpoches, lamas, and gurus of our time. My decades of study and daily practice have allowed me to cultivate a real-world teaching regimen to help others find balance, heal themselves, awaken the Divine, and transform as they integrate these sacred powers into their own hearts, homes, work environments, and relationships.

These Sacred Powers are infused with the divine flow of the Universe, the very same stardust that moves all life to its highest vibration. And they have the ability—if you embrace them—to gracefully and effortlessly shift your life from where it is to where you'd like to be, to raise *your* vibration as you move throughout the world.

EVERYTHING IS ENERGY

Resting at the timeless core of these principles has always been a profound belief in and a deep reverence for the power of energy: the life force that flows through every molecule of existence, often called "the breath of the universe." The ancient Chinese, Japanese, and Indian cultures referred to it as *chi*, *Qi*, *prana*, and *Shakti*. In Africa, it was called *ashe*; in ancient Egypt, *ka*; in Hawai'i, *mana*; and in ancient Greek, *pneuma*.

But energy is not simply present in the physical and material world outside us. Yes. It's in our bodies through the air we breathe, the food we eat, the stars we gaze at in the night sky, and even our subtle response to solar flares happening right now on the sun. But it's also in our thoughts, the words we choose, the conversations we have, the feelings in our minds and hearts, and the ripple that continues from each of our interactions like the waves on an ocean 10,000 miles away. That same energy flows through our very essence as energetic expressions of life. The breath of the universe is contained in *our every* thought, desire, choice, word, and action.

WE ARE BEINGS OF TRANSFORMATION

Modern science says that the energy existing in our world today is the exact same amount of energy that has existed since the beginning of time more than 13 billion years ago. Albert Einstein confirmed this in the 1950s when he wrote, "Energy cannot be created or destroyed; it can only be changed from one form to another."

Let that settle in for a moment.

Energy cannot be created or destroyed. It can only be changed from one form to another. We call this shape-shifting of energy *transformation*.

We transform the world by transforming ourselves. And by joining me on this magnificent journey, you've already taken a powerful energetic step toward your own personal transformation. Take a deep breath. The best is yet to come. Once the Sacred Powers are awakened within you, they will be carried forever in an energetic flow that will touch and transform everyone you interact with for all eternity. So together, let's explore these Five Divine Paths, unlock their eternal secrets, weave some stardust into your life, begin living the Five Divine Principles, and awaken your *Sacred Powers of Transformation*.

The First Secret

THE
DIVINE PRINCIPLE
OF ONE

The Divine Principle of One
and
The Sacred Powers of Presence,
Your Ripple, and Spirit

CHAPTER TWO

WALKING THE FIRST DIVINE PATH

The Journey Begins

Every day is a journey, and the journey itself is home.

— Matsuo Bashō

The *Divine Principle of One* is a natural law of the Universe . . . absolute, incontrovertible, and undeniable. All other laws of physics, math, science, and spirit spring from this defining principle of existence. There is only One—and yet there is an infinite amount of its expression in our world—way beyond the nearly eight billion people who populate the planet. The divine thumbprint of the Universe rests embedded inside every particle, gust of wind, drop of water, blade of grass, and ray of light. Whatever floats, flies, swims, crawls, sits, walks, or grows is birthed from that one source that began it all. Right now, the Universe is breathing life through every micron of existence in some form or another. You are a magnificent and unique expression of this divine breath, flowing one-ness in every moment. And, yet, so often we look at our lives through a lens of separation, rarely recognizing the common threads that are woven through every aspect of our realities.

UNDERSTANDING OUR ONE-NESS

When you look at the world from the viewpoint of your own individuality, it's easy to see yourself as a meaningless speck in the
vastness of existence. Drill down farther and you are just one person out of the billions who populate earth. When you go even
deeper still, there are times when you believe that it's just you, all
alone. Sometimes it can be difficult to comprehend where we fit
in the divine scheme of things. And this is often because at some
level, we believe that our lives consist of our bodies, our thoughts,
and our beliefs.

We think about our existence in earthbound terms, believing
that we *are* our bodies and our thoughts. But we are both and we
are neither. Yes, you *have* a body—it's reading these words and
chemically processing them into ideas. And you *have* thoughts—
almost one very second—and they are merging with the parades
of other thoughts that continue to flow into your awareness. But
you are not your body, and you are not your thoughts. You are
pure, unbounded light being expressed through your physical
body and your thoughts, which then move your body to act in
different ways. You are a human *being*, and as the embodiment
of *being*, your essence is timeless, formless, guided only by Five
Divine Principles of timeless, formless, boundless understanding:

- *The Divine Principle of One*

- *The Divine Principle of Awareness*

- *The Divine Principle of REbirth*

- *The Divine Principle of Infinite Flow*

- *The Divine Principle of Inner Fire*

Awakening to such a cosmic revelation at this stage of your
life, after you've been taught that you are simply your body and
your thoughts—and after decades of reinforcement in every millisecond of your life from the very moment you came out of the
womb—is mind-blowing. I get it. But this is how pure, magnificent transformation takes hold. And whether you feel it or not—as

10

all of your old mind-sets, constrictions, and limiting beliefs continue to melt away like veils concealing your divine core—you are powerfully transforming.

ONE-NESS IS WHOLENESS

As you lie awake in your bed at night, gazing at the ceiling, even if there is another person or animal lying next to you, it's so easy to feel separate, even lonely. But loneliness and aloneness are two very different concepts. When you are lonely, you are in a prison of sorts, feeling the pain of your separation. You yearn for another being to help you feel whole, another voice to listen to, another face to gaze upon, another body to feel, another person to soothe your aching feeling of estrangement.

When you are truly alone, you are whole—fully integrated into everything, liberated from your need to cling to another, released from any longing, and finally free to experience the ecstasy of your one-ness. In your wholeness, your Sacred Powers are fully awakened, and you have infinite choices at your fingertips that are not driven by some need to feel completed by another. In a state of true aloneness, joy is reawakened, your sense of divinity is restored, and you feel totally at home in your own skin— and delighted with your circumstance. When you are in a state of divine aloneness, you can choose to either isolate yourself or connect with another, to surrender to your own magnificence or commune with someone else's.

DIVINE OPPORTUNITIES

Aloneness creates the opportunity to make truly conscious, unconditioned choices. When you are lonely, you have only one dimension—craving another person or thing outside yourself to make you happy. When you are alone, you are multidimensional, with the source of all happiness flowing from within. In a state of aloneness, there is no sense of yearning—but rather an understanding of your wholeness. And so your desire is not to "complete" yourself by seeking anything or anyone outside of yourself, but to simply allow your true essence to unfold from within.

In that moment, your aloneness is sweet solitude. Never confuse loneliness with aloneness. Aloneness offers the opportunity for profound understanding, expanding self-discovery, and an appreciation of your divine one-ness with all of existence. Aloneness is an opportunity for deep reverence—a chance to drop to your knees in gratitude, and kiss the earth with love—and also the opportunity for a magnificent celebration that the grace of the Universe flows from within you.

THE JOURNEY OF ALONENESS

Those on a spiritual journey often struggle with the pain of feeling separate. They have been out there in the world slaying dragons, and suddenly they come in direct contact with the whispers of the Universe telling them to go deeper. These divine murmurs shadow them throughout the day, creating a form of conflict between everything they've ever been taught about life and the new sensations and perspectives they are suddenly feeling, contemplating, and experiencing. And as they begin to delve more deeply into a passion play of two distinct realities, they are faced with massive incongruities regarding how they suddenly see the world and where they find their place in it.

This is why people are unexpectedly sparked onto spiritual journeys after they've lived a full and substantial life. And once they've gotten their first taste of a sublime moment, they realize that *there is* something more, a new magnificent life they never even dreamed they could live. In their aha moments, they often say, "If only I had learned this as a child, I would have . . ." or "If I knew then what I know now, I never would have . . ." But the truth is, you are never ready until the moment you are truly *ready*. And if you've made it this far with me, *you* are distinctly ready. Now is your time, and most likely, you are already feeling the shift. The reality is that these teachings probably wouldn't have made any sense to you way back then. And even if you had understood them, it wouldn't have mattered. Timing is everything. And, feeling your divine one-ness can occur only when the time is right.

YOU ARE THAT

The one-ness of our existence is evident in every moment. We are not simply part of a collective of BEings. We are the same being. Your breath is my breath, your heartbeat is my heartbeat, your pain is my pain, and your triumphs are mine as well. With so many people on the planet, it's often impossible to comprehend that you share the essence of a tribal warrior 10,000 miles away. Or that your soul and the soul of some violent dictator in another country are one. But at your core, you are whole and one with everything in existence and everything that *has* ever existed. You are also one with the greatest healers, lovers, activists, and peaceful warriors who have ever lived. You are one with the most magnificent scientists, leaders, and businesspeople, who've transformed the world; you are one with the greatest visionaries, artists, and philosophers who have ever walked the planet. Our one-ness is our birthright, the very core of our being, and the divine light that guides us through our personal evolution.

WHO AM I?

We try to figure this out every day by making comparisons to better understand who we are. We are in constant judgment mode of everything around us to help figure out our emotions, beliefs, and attitudes. We clarify our world by separating from the one-ness that binds us too closely to things we don't approve of. When a politician says something that rocks us to our core, we say to ourselves, "That's not me!" You overhear a conversation between a parent and child, and the tone of the encounter doesn't sit well with you, so you establish in your heart, "That's not me!" We move throughout the day judging and assessing everything inside us and outside us to determine who we are and where we stand on everything from the car we drive, to the toilet paper we use, to the food we eat. We base our belief systems, our diets, our causes, and even our most mundane likes and dislikes from a point of view that we are these individual bags of molecules, sealed in this flesh casing for the span of a lifetime.

MIRROR, MIRROR

In each moment, we bring things closer that feel good or "right" and distance ourselves from that which makes us feel icky or wrong. And because we are continuously individuating ourselves on a physical and emotional level, we have learned to interpret the entire world around us as separate from ourselves. The timeless wisdom of the *Divine Principle of One* reminds us in every moment that we are merely a reflection of everything we see, hear, touch, taste, smell, feel, and think. We co-create every situation that we celebrate and every scenario that we ridicule. And when we find ourselves judging, criticizing, or condemning someone in our life, it means we have forgotten our foundation of Oneness—we are denying that we share the same essence as the person we disparage.

One of the least understood, yet most powerful, aspects of the *Divine Principle of One* is the concept of sacred wholeness. This ancient teaching was a hallmark of the unshakeable inclusiveness of Jesus, the unfathomable compassion of the Buddha, and the unwavering nonviolence of Martin Luther King, Jr. These sages truly understood the concept of the whole and all its pieces. Jesus fought fear with trust; Buddha fought suffering with love; and Martin Luther King fought injustice with peace. This ancient teaching has been lost on many misguided modern-day activists, politicians, and spiritual teachers, who have regrettably become voices of hate in their quests to advance trust, love, and peace. That's why it is so critical that you and I embrace the concept of sacred wholeness and live it even more deeply.

SACRED WHOLENESS AND PERSONAL WHOLENESS

The *Divine Principle of One* ripples through every aspect of our being, infusing all of our thoughts, words, and actions with the eternal wisdom of sacred wholeness. We are all part of the whole. The wholeness of existence contains a magnificent fusion of opposing—yet complementary—forces that are in dynamic exchange in every moment to create the totality of the Universe: fire and water; expansion and contraction; strength and weakness; abundance and poverty; pleasure and pain; surrender and fury; resistance and acceptance; suffering and compassion; humility and arrogance; hate and love; violence and peace; fear and trust; and darkness and light. All the pieces of existence must be present in order for there to be balance in the cosmos.

Since everything in existence contains the essence of wholeness, everything contains both darkness and light. When you see darkness in others, that is also part of the whole. The moment we feel dragged down by the darkness of another person, the ancient wisdom encourages us to make a more conscious choice toward raising our own vibration and intensifying our own light. The *Divine Principle of One* is all about the union of all things—it teaches us that in our quest for wholeness, we counter hate with love, emotional turbulence with calm, lethargy with energy, despair with encouragement, and darkness with light.

Speaking to us on many levels, the *Divine Principle of One:*

- Guides, inspires, and teaches us about life in every moment

- Illuminates our path, points the way, and helps us navigate each step of our journey

- Expands our understanding of the pure, unbounded infinity of the Universe

- Provides us with profound insights into the true nature of the sacred essence that rests at our very core

The *Divine Principle of One* has existed for eternity infusing virtually every philosophy, religion, family, community, and nation on earth with its most sacred value and core belief—*we are all one.* There are millions of ways to express that one-ness, but it's the undeniable foundation for all existence. Our physical bodies work that way; our minds as well; the family structure you grew up in; and the town you live in; all the way up to the Universe in its very first stardust moment. An obvious example is the Latin motto for the United States of America: *E Pluribus Unum*—which means "out of many, one." And there are three Sacred Powers that have upheld this timeless truth of one-ness since that very first stardust explosion:

- *The Sacred Power of Presence*
- *The Sacred Power of Your Ripple*
- *The Sacred Power of Spirit*

Awakening them connects you to the one-ness that rests inside, the one-ness that unites you with everything else on the planet, and the eternal union of your soul and the divine Spirit.

CHAPTER THREE

THE SACRED POWER
OF PRESENCE

*Whatever has happened to you in the past
has no power over this present moment, because life is now.*

— Oprah Winfrey

From the moment we crept out of the womb, we have been on an unconscious mission to separate ourselves from the one-ness of existence. We rarely take the time to connect to our Source. We are pulled and prodded, yanked and invited, teased and distracted by the merry-go-round of everything outside of our soul. We rarely make time to truly connect with our breath. We seldom stop to smell the roses—or any flowers at all. We often don't seize the moment and look around at the lips of people or gaze into their eyes or listen to the sounds of their breathing. We often look right through them and just say what we need to say without watching our words unfold in their minds—and in most cases others aren't listening either as they prepare their next sentence in response.

We view the present moment as a potential interruption between what we were doing and what we *could* be doing. We use phrases like "carve out time," "make time," and "squeeze it in," as if time was this separate entity that was always imposing itself on us. We often postpone the occasion to be fully present with those near and dear to us. We multitask our love, fragmenting our affection over several people and things simultaneously. We often hold back an innocent expression of kindness for fear of it being misinterpreted. We keep our distance because we don't know what to do with that empty space where connection flows. And yet we are all just stumbling in the darkness of loneliness begging for someone to light a match. We've grown so accustomed to seeing ourselves as individual beings that we often rationalize our isolation as being normal.

Were we so traumatized when we were pulled from our mothers' wombs to begin our journey of individuation? Is the human condition one of mass separation anxiety that clouds our true nature of wholeness? Have we bought into some grand hallucination? Even Albert Einstein viewed this unique phenomenon of man's self-imposed personal exile as "a kind of optical delusion of his consciousness." He echoed the guidance of the *Divine Principle of One*, when he suggested we "free ourselves from this prison by widening our circle of compassion to embrace all living creatures and the whole of nature in its beauty." Einstein was speaking about the *Sacred Power of Presence*—our path back to wholeness.

In our current world, where everything is on-demand, we rarely infuse presence into the soundtrack of our life. Yet no song could truly exist unless there was a space between the notes being played or the words being sung. Presence is the powerful stillness and silence that already exists before activity arises. It is there before and after every thought, word, and action. But we rarely acknowledge it or celebrate it. Instead, we rationalize it away by filling those spaces with more activity. And yet the present moment is actually the *only* thing we have.

Compared to the eternity of the cosmos, this physical life of ours is as short as a flash of lightning. We will all leave this earthly existence at some point. That alone should inspire us to celebrate our own presence right now—and that of everyone in our lives. But that *optical delusion of our consciousness* clouds each moment instead, distracting us from our one-ness. Awakening the *Sacred Power of Presence* in your life encourages you to drink in every moment, to recognize that feeling separate from the whole is an illusion, and to seize the moment or as Henry David Thoreau advised, "to live deliberately . . . to live deep and suck out all the marrow of life," because our next breath on this earth is promised to no one.

OUR BEST VERSION

We would like to believe that the emotions we reserve for our loved ones are always heart based, encouraging, and kind. The reality is that we often take those we love for granted. I am not judging your life here. I'm sure your intentions are to always shower those closest to you with the greatest amount of attention and care, but we frequently reserve that treatment for those who *don't* really know us intimately—people we've just met, clients, customers, vendors, new relationships—as we try to make the best impression.

Have you ever snapped at a loved one after having a tough time or a difficult encounter, even though it had nothing to do with them? Have you inadvertently been snide, sarcastic, snarky, retaliatory, biting, or downright mean to someone you love who had little or nothing to do with your initial frustration? When was the last time you were texting or staring at your device while someone you care about was talking to you? When was the last time you got frustrated or irritated with someone you love simply because they were encroaching on your mental space? When was the last time you were someplace else in your mind while you were spending "quality time" with a loved one? When was the last time you were impatient with a loved one when they did not deserve it?

EVIDENCE OF PRESENCE

Think of all the times you felt anger from seeing a loved one's unwashed dishes in the sink, the cap off the toothpaste, or their clothes strewn about the room. Would you have gotten as irritated if you knew they were soon going to die? Well, they will one day. And as difficult as it may be for you to even think about, the reality is that we all will die one day. With the knowledge that those in your life are finite and will one day leave this earthly realm, shouldn't the evidence of their presence in this world make you hug them instead of scold them? Shouldn't we fondly smile when we trip over their shoes left out in plain sight knowing that one day those shoes will be neatly positioned on the floor of a closet, never to be worn again?

Evidence of presence can be our mantra when we are about to reach out to someone with anything other than love. Using it as a watchword can remind us how fleeting this existence is and how precious our time with them truly is. So right now, let's reach out to someone we love with a text or e-mail that simply says, "Thinking of you and sending love." Don't make it complicated. Just type those words right now and hit send.

The next time you start to get frustrated from a loved one's presence, hug them instead and see how that shifts your emotional state. And throughout each day, the moment you start to feel your body constricting with irritation, silently say to yourself, *Evidence of presence*, and allow feelings of love to ripple into your heart. The *Sacred Power of Presence* is a constant exercise in loving what is and celebrating those who share this flickering of a moment in time and space.

CONNECTING TO THE PRESENT MOMENT

As we awaken the *Sacred Power of Presence* within us, we are gently guided back to the stillness and silence that rests inside, back to a state of being where there is time for everything.

For thousands of years, the ancient oracles, shamans, sages, and seers practiced and ultimately mastered the *Sacred Power of Presence* in their lives. And although it's not very complicated, in our modern world where mindfulness and meditation are readily available to all, most people still have not cultivated a present-moment technique that they engage in every day.

The ancient Chinese sage Lao-tzu is known for this powerful set of teachings, which reinforce the *Sacred Power of Presence*:

> Do you have the patience to wait
> until your mud settles and the water is clear?

Can you remain unmoving
till the right action arises by itself?

The Master doesn't seek fulfillment:
but not seeking, not expecting,
is fully present,
and can welcome all things.

As the swirl of life sweeps through you each day, allow these three powerful stanzas to become an ongoing contemplation. Gently rippling them through your thoughts will help you gain clarity, cultivate patience, and trust in the moment.

The ancient masters of meditation didn't use apps or spa music to connect them to the present moment. They embraced the *Divine Principle of One* so purely, building their lives around daily present-moment practices, that they were able to effortlessly awaken the *Sacred Power of Presence*. They infused their whole day into their present moments as opposed to inserting occasional presence into their day. Buddha did not try to "squeeze" a meditation in between meetings, and the Bible is filled with references to Jesus praying throughout the day as part of his sacred devotion.

Cultivating a daily present-moment practice is much easier than you may think. And if we can accept the excuses of "no time" or "too busy" for exactly what they are—*excuses* (and lame ones at that)—then we can begin to integrate presence into our life and create a magnificent fusion of a fully present existence. We know you weren't too busy to send that text, "Thinking of you and sending love," but if you did make some kind of excuse, stop reading now, and make sending that text your present-moment activity!

PRACTICING PRESENCE

At first, "finding the time" to practice presence may feel like a chore, but this is the natural progression we all go through on our journey to stillness. The easiest way to connect with the flow more effortlessly is to practice throughout the day while you're stuck in traffic, standing in a line, sitting in the bathroom, attending a meeting, or even taking a shower. You can start out with an easy technique that requires no equipment called "16 seconds." I've taught it to more than 200,000 people around the world, and it's based on the ancient technique of mindful breathing popularized by the Buddha 2,600 years ago.

> Start with a long, slow, deep inhale through your nose, and watch your breath slowly move into you and follow it down deep into your belly; then hold the breath in and witness it as it sits in your belly. Release your breath, and observe it as it moves back up, through you, and out of your nostrils. As you continue to exhale, watch your breath as you continue releasing it out, and observing it the whole time as it dissipates into the air. In. Hold. Out. Hold. Witnessing the whole time as you move through this simple four-part breathing technique. Each component takes about 4 seconds, with the whole experience lasting 16 seconds. You can approximate your time by counting along the way, or simply surrender to the process and see where it leads you. Sixteen seconds is all it takes to practice presence. And you can gently increase your presence practice to a minute by doing it 4 times, or to 5 minutes by doing it 20 times.

This time-tested process will instantly infuse all the conversations in your head with a tiny bit of stillness. The resulting newfound clarity in your mind will then start to subliminally pervade your choice-making as your laser focus guides you in ways you never thought were possible. This concentrated light of single-mindedness cuts through the fog of indecision, pierces the veils of confusion, and brings an instant settling down of emotions that would otherwise succumb to melodrama. Your tranquil inner dialogue evolves into a calmer and more composed outer dialogue. The swirl around you slows, creating an inviting aura of tranquility that others appreciate participating in. And as all of your interactions start to proceed at a slower speed, you receive information more clearly, process it more objectively, and speak with greater poise and purpose.

THE SIX STAGES OF A PRESENT-MOMENT EXPERIENCE

Every present-moment experience contains a six-stage evolution: *Settling, Witnessing, Drifting, Judging, Surrendering,* and *Stillness.* The key to cultivating a regular and consistent practice of presence in your life is your ability to fully accept and understand that this is exactly what the experience is supposed to be.

Settling—Comfort is queen. To begin any practice, we must first find a comfortable place to settle in, which could be a chair, a couch, a car seat, the floor, a toilet seat, or a closet. We find that space and get as comfortable as possible. And then we gently close our eyes. This helps us eliminate as many distractions as possible—those we might see with our eyes and any we might feel with our body. Then we take a long, slow, deep breath in through our nose, and then gently let it go. Try it now. Let's do it one more time. Feel that release? This is how we settle in.

Witnessing—We continue breathing slowly and gently. And as our breathing continues, we begin to watch our breath as it moves in and as it moves out. We simply observe it; witness it flow in and back out. We don't strain or try. We don't squint and focus. We simply stay in the space of observing, witnessing, and watching. Every time you simply witness, you strengthen your ability to stay in that state longer and more easily.

Drifting—After holding our attention for an extended period of time on anything, it is natural that we drift toward thoughts, sounds, and physical sensations. Even gazing at the most beautiful painting sets our attention adrift. We may find ourselves having conversations, replaying past events, making lists, fidgeting, feeling restless, or simply experiencing a flow of random thoughts. This is totally natural since we have trained ourselves to forever be drifting backward into the past and forward into the future. It means that you are alive, and, like any healthy human walking the planet, your brain is doing what it has been trained to do—processing thoughts.

Judging—Somewhere along the way, you bought into the false notion that a present-moment experience was supposed to be a blissed-out Zen experience filled with peace and light, and perhaps even some angel whispering in your ear. That's why suddenly finding yourself making a shopping list in the middle of your practice has you thinking you're doing it wrong. The perfectionist in you starts to battle what's going on inside, and you begin to judge your practice. You evaluate and criticize the way you're sitting, the thoughts flowing into you, the way you're breathing, and anything else you might be doing to get in the way of nirvana.

Surrendering—When you notice that you are scolding yourself for a less-than-perfect experience, remind yourself to just relax. Humans have about 70,000 thoughts a day—or about one every second. That's a lot of thoughts. The greatest meditators who have ever lived have thoughts when they meditate. So why wouldn't you? After we've judged ourselves for not "doing it right," it's time to let go, settle down, and drift back to witnessing. Once you have accepted the fact that drifting and judging are natural aspects of the process, you can fully surrender.

Stillness—As you get more comfortable gently drifting back and forth, you'll start to spend a little more time in *witness land* and a little less time in *thought land*. You will have cultivated your ability to witness, and you will have awakened the *Sacred Power of Presence*. And every time you visit the land of witnessing, you bring back into your waking world a thimbleful of stillness that gently infuses all of your thoughts, words, and actions.

As with any presence practice, you simply start by settling in, then you'll begin to witness, and over time you'll become aware that you've drifted away. When you notice yourself judging, grant yourself permission to be human and have thoughts. You can even remind yourself, "I'm having thoughts. That means I'm alive!" Then surrender back into witnessing, and soon you'll feel stillness. Once this time-tested practice takes on a larger role in your life—either for 16 seconds or longer—you'll begin to feel a little bit of presence in every moment, without you really having to do anything else differently in your life.

If you don't have a daily practice of presence, start with 16 seconds, and make the commitment to expand your practice by one minute a week. Take it slow and steady. You can also visit davidji.com, where I have hundreds of free guided meditations to help you cultivate your *Sacred Power of Presence*.

The *Divine Principle of One* encourages us to weave the present moment into every aspect of our being and because we are creatures of connection, we can begin to effortlessly transform the world around us *with our own presence* through the *Sacred Power of Your Ripple*.

CHAPTER FOUR

THE SACRED POWER OF YOUR RIPPLE

*All you have to do is touch the right key
at the right time and the instrument will play itself.*

— Johann Sebastian Bach

Each of us has the ability to raise our vibration, flow that energy out into the world, and live a truly magnificent life. But as we move throughout the day, stubbing our toes, taking things personally, holding on to grievances, feeling less than, and playing small—we instead show up in predictable, conditioned expressions. When we can truly grasp the expansiveness inside of us, and the impact we have on thousands of people each day—then the power of our ripple takes on new meaning with our thoughts, our words, and our actions flowing infinitely throughout time. Awakening the *Sacred Power of Your Ripple* will help you step into your power, own your impact, and transform the world around you.

COSMIC COMMUNION

One-ness is at the core of our existence. You and I—and everything that exists in our lives—are all made up of that same stardust that first birthed our world. As conduits of the Universe, we receive the breath of the Universe and vibrate it back out with thoughts, words, and actions that express our uniqueness. Think of the infinite number of interactions that needed to occur for you and me to be sitting right here connecting to each other. The millions of decisions that each of us have made, the billions of actions that others in our life have taken to coordinate this communion, and the trillions of choices that people we don't even know have made to divinely conspire that you and I would share this sacred, precious present moment.

It's truly unfathomable. But if any of those people had simply turned left instead of right, at some intersection 10,000 miles away from here, none of it would have transpired the way it has. Change one thread in the cosmic fabric of our life, and the whole pattern changes, everything shifts, the trajectory is altered, the journey veers off in a totally different direction, and the outcome will be light-years from what it otherwise might have been.

Reflecting back on my conversation with the Nadi Palm Leaf Reader so many years ago, one of the amazing cosmic revelations he revealed to me was that you and I have been rippling for eternity. For thousands of years, we have been taking steps, making choices, and dancing together throughout the "jungles of time and space" as my dear friend Mike Dooley calls them in his *Notes from the Universe*. Your life has extreme and magnificent meaning. And we both have been summoned by the Universe to this very moment in a never-ending cosmic story to transform the world as we transform ourselves. That's why the *Sacred Power of Your Ripple* is so profound.

We are rippling in every moment as the Universe relentlessly feeds our minds a thought every second. In response, we translate them into our next moment as we bend, lean, sigh, laugh, crystallize, and transform them in some way. We are rippling like innocent bees flitting from flower to flower, unaware we are pollinating every new blossom as we go about our day sipping nectar.

Stop right now and think about all the people you interacted with this week—those you barely remember and those with whom you have had a deeper connection. Every one of them experienced your vibration in some way. And although it's only been a few minutes, by now you've probably received a reply to your text,

"Thinking of you and sending love." What did it say? What was the response? What was the impact of those six little words you effortlessly shared? This is the *Sacred Power of Your Ripple* in action! If you'd like to share it and fully validate your sacred power, e-mail me at info@davidji.com, and I'll reply to you so we can keep the energy flowing! Use the subject line "Rippling."

IMPACT

Every time we think, speak, or act, we are influencing the flow of energy. The quality of our relationships modulates how we perceive the world—and how those around us perceive what we have to share with them. We have no control over the ripple once it leaves us, which is why being impeccable with your ripple is so critical. The receiver of your earlier text sending your love is most likely being rippled with some sort of happiness. Maybe they were feeling low, and this elevated them. Maybe they were missing you, and seeing your words made them feel complete. Maybe you weren't in their mind at all, and now you are. Maybe they were in the middle of doing something time sensitive, and your text irritated them, so they swiped it aside. Every being on the planet is playing a cosmic game of tag, rippling energy into the atmosphere, impacting the environment, influencing the thoughts of others, and showering their vibrations throughout the world in a nonstop symphony.

Some call it *impact*, and others refer to it as *legacy*. Each of us is painting the world every day with our legacy. What have you painted the world with today? What paintbrush and color palette have you used, and what message did you send? In every moment, we are making the tiniest of brush strokes. We see it in the sparkle in the eye of a cashier when you say, "Thank you" to the sense of relief on the face of another driver when you wave them in front of you in a line of traffic to the ease that settles in when you tell the customer service person you're dealing with that they are really helping you out.

Complaints, grievances, and scowls are ever flowing in our world. But respect, praise, compliments, and expressions of appreciation are in short supply. The *Sacred Power of Your Ripple* teaches you in every moment to pay attention to what you are leaving behind in each moment, because long after you've left the scene, your impact remains. The next time you walk or drive away from someplace, ask yourself, "Did I just leave the scene of a crime, or did I just add value to the moment?" The vibration of the world elevates with every positive ripple you add. And, obviously, it declines with every negative ripple you put out there. Negative ripples entirely erase positive ones. No matter how hard you've tried in the past to flow kindness, one negative ripple and *poof!* It's all undone.

THE RIPPLE OF YOUR RELATIONSHIPS

Exploring the *Sacred Power of Your Ripple* is a profound exercise when you think about how many diverse relationships you have in your life. And whether you are close with someone, never speak with them, or have a challenging relationship, you are holding on to mental and emotional energy regarding the current status of the connection. The starting point for all ripples is the relationship you have with yourself. How do you treat yourself? How's your sense of self-worth? Are you arrogant, condescending, and mean to yourself? Or loving, forgiving, nurturing, and compassionate? Do you flow unconditional love? Or are you in constant comparison mode? Where do you really stand in your mind's eye? That is the seed of every single ripple in your life.

As you expand the circle beyond yourself, ask, "Who's in my front row?" Essentially, who are your die-hard supporters, your cheerleaders, and your champions? Those are the relationships you should be placing the most attention on. But are you? When you stumble, who is rooting for you to get back up? Are there people in your *front row* who don't belong there? Do you rationalize that because someone is a relative of yours, you are willing to compromise your self-worth? Are there people in your circle of friends or relatives who just seem to be taking up space, blocking new champions from taking *their* seats in your front row? We let people into our heads that we would never invite into our homes.

And yet there they are, sitting firmly on their hands in the best seats in the house, when everyone else in the theater is on their feet and applauding you.

Close your eyes with your hand on your heart, and widen the circle even farther to include everyone you can think of and envision them filling seats in the theater of your life. Who's in your front row? The second row? The next row? Are there people taking up space who probably could be moved back a few rows to make room for someone else? Are there those who probably should be moved to another theater? Are there people rooting for you that you haven't made space for? Now envision what your ideal theater looks like. Envision your view from the stage, where every face you see is cheering, rooting for you, and on your side.

FOUR WAYS YOUR RELATIONSHIPS RIPPLE

When it comes to your relationships, the *Sacred Power of Your Ripple* manifests in your life in four ways:

1. **Birthing a New Relationship.** We begin the journey with our highest hopes and infinite possibilities. This is where the seed is planted and every thought, word, and interaction then builds on the fabric of the relationship rippling it to a unique vibration. We can tend to it lovingly and commit to evolving it in every moment by being fully present and never taking it for granted.

2. **Repairing a Fractured Relationship.** A wounding or lack of attention at a pivotal moment can cause a relationship to fracture. If you desire to keep the relationship alive and get it back on track, then both parties must agree to let go of the past actions and their ripple. They need to forgive each other completely, commit to soothing wounds, and let go of any grievances. Both parties need to recommit to making new ripples of healing, dedicating their time, attention, and effort to the mission of returning the

relationship to wholeness. If only one person desires this newly energized rippling, then repairing is not an option. If bilateral commitment is not possible, then the next option is Shifting.

3. **Shifting and Starting Anew.** Relationships evolve all the time. Maybe you are taking a platonic relationship to an intimate place, or you once were close and you need to step back a bit. Or perhaps now you have a work relationship with a friend or have become friendly with a work colleague. Maybe the other person isn't expressing themselves in the same way that first brought you together. Or perhaps they've become physically, emotionally, or mentally frail, such as with an aging parent.

   Whatever the reason, the old way isn't working in the current environment, but you still want to be connected at some level then new boundaries, understandings, and rules of engagement must be articulated and committed to by both parties. Everyone involved has to be willing to dedicate themselves to the new, agreed-on dynamic where the old dreams, desires, and expectations no longer apply. Sometimes this is the last gasp on the way to the relationship graveyard. But if the willingness and dedication are there, then a magnificent new platform can be constructed with fresh dreams, desires, and expectations that both of you can embrace, nourish, and reinforce. If you have given your all, and new terms of engagement can't be agreed on, or one of you continues to hold a grudge, then most likely you need to agree to formally end it.

4. **Ending a Relationship.** Perhaps the time has come to cut the cord, say good-bye, and let go of what no longer serves either of you. But, as we know, energy can never be created or destroyed. It can only be transformed, and it continues to ripple in eternity,

which is why the concept of closure can be so challenging. If this is where you find yourself, now is the time to awaken compassion—self-compassion and compassion for the other person. If you've tried to make it work, but it brings more pain than joy, then starting with an open, forgiving, compassionate heart is the *only* way to move forward. If you harbor bitterness, anger, or vengeance, these toxic emotions will harden your heart, hinder your ability to love again, and get in the way of new relationships.

If your desire is to *truly* let it go and move on, then remove all traces of them in your life—remove the *evidence of their presence*. Every day release one more piece of the relationship, and redirect your energy to another more nourishing relationship.

The *Divine Principle of One* teaches that nothing on this earth ever really ends; we must make peace in our own hearts, forgive ourselves, forgive them, and the key to this is to release, release, release. Forgiveness has very little to do with the other person—it comes from within. The ancient teachings remind us that when we forgive, we free ourselves from the threads that connect us to the one who hurt us. So start to loosen your grip on those threads.

THE RIPPLES OF YOUR HEART

The *Sacred Power of Your Ripple* is fueled by four basic needs that are in constant dynamic exchange as we move through our lives—*attention, affection, appreciation,* and *acceptance*. Every day, we consciously and unconsciously flow these ripples out into the world and receive them back in an infinite give-and-take that determines how we feel about ourselves, how others feel about us, how we interact with the world around us, and how it interacts with us. These four *ripples of the heart* set the tone for every encounter you will ever experience—with yourself, others, and the environment.

Attention

We all want to be seen. We all want to be looked at. We struggle so hard to receive eye contact even if it's fleeting. This is where we get validated for simply existing. We sense it. We value it. We need it. And everyone you interact with needs it too. Attention is the starting point for the *Sacred Power of Your Ripple*. It's the "I see you" moment.

Affection

A bit deeper than attention is *affection*. We all want to receive a physical display of that validation—a wink, a nod, a smile, a hug, a kiss, a squeeze, or a kind word. It distills that distant attention we crave down to a level of closeness, where we experience someone's warmth or fondness for us. The *Sacred Power of Your Ripple* has the ability to flow affection throughout the world at the basic level of kindness and the deeper expression of love.

Appreciation

One step deeper than affection is *appreciation*—moving from a kind word or gesture to genuine gratitude. We all want to be thanked, recognized, and acknowledged. We all want to feel that we have added value to the moment, task, project, or mission at hand. Appreciation is more overt or public acknowledgment of a good deed, a job well done, or an important contribution. And yet it can be as simple as a "thank you" from a stranger when you hold open the door for them. When you demonstrate appreciation, you elevate another's sense of self-worth. Miraculously, this also elevates your own!

Areas of our life where we don't feel appreciated cause us extreme struggle and result in a wide range of emotions. Right now there is probably something you worked hard on, or a gift you gave someone, and you did not receive the thanks or gratitude you were expecting. And now it haunts you. This little irritant resting under the surface can influence and impact your daily anxiety, anger, or irritation. Multiply that by the thousands of little ripples you are sending out into the world, and you can see the impact of the *Sacred Power of Your Ripple* on every relationship in your life.

We are rippling in every moment. Humans are totally dependent on the feedback of their friends, siblings, parents, teachers, co-workers, bosses, and everyone else with whom they come into contact. Every decision we make is done with the hope of some level of acknowledgment that we've added value. Every one of us still craves the ripple of appreciation. It's our external validator that we are connected to and making a difference in the lives of others. If we don't receive that validation, it can scar us forever. And when you don't flow the ripple of appreciation, it can wound another eternally as well. Why not say how you feel? What's the worst that could happen? What's the best that could happen?

Acceptance

Our need for acceptance drives so many of our daily and life decisions. We need to feel the ripple of someone or something bigger than us. We crave this acceptance—in the grandest ways and in the smallest moments. Being invited, included, and, most importantly, *being welcomed* relentlessly influence our sense of worthiness. When we were younger, we based our self-worth on whether we were accepted into various groups based on our internal assessment of how cool, relevant, or popular the group was. That hasn't changed. Our need for support and respect *from those we respect* can be a powerful driving force in our lives. Nowadays, we do this with our affiliations to schools, clubs, sports teams, religious groups, social media, political parties, nationalities, ethnicities, and cultures—it's all about being accepted. Many of us crave acceptance so deeply that we secretly value being accepted *by people we don't even like!*

When we don't "feel" acceptance, we spend a lot of time stuck in "poor me" mode, where the power of our ripple slows to a drip. We respond to the world by feeling "less-than"—we isolate ourselves, act desperate, or behave resentfully regarding our lack of inclusion. In time this devolves into an antagonistic and ultimately victimized attitude where our ripple stops entirely. We can spend decades trapped in the world of not feeling accepted.

So when we don't receive the attention, affection, appreciation, or acceptance that is our birthright, we feel shame, anger, jealousy, schadenfreude (delighting in someone else's struggle), even vengeance. That's putting a lot of power in the hands of others. But, even worse, it paints the seed of your ripple with desperate or negative vibrations. Feeling accepted and demonstrating acceptance of others elevates you to a higher vibration of positivity and reinforces your humanity.

YOUR VOICE

The *Sacred Power of Your Ripple* flows through infinity, but it starts with you. Why would you expect someone else to be accepting of you, if you don't fully accept yourself? We need to make a daily commitment to accept ourselves in every moment, be kind to ourselves, and appreciate ourselves. That's truly the only validation we need. And this begins with you truly understanding your voice.

When we think of our voice, we often view it as the words that come out of our mouth. But this is just the vibration of our vocal cords. Your voice is much more expansive than simply words—it's the energy you flow in every moment and the ripple of that energy. We "speak" in verbal and nonverbal ways—from the choices we've made to the messages we send—to the divine purpose that holds our stars apart and our Universe together.

Some of us have dimmed our light over fear of being diminished by another—biting our tongues or walking on eggshells because we don't have the confidence to risk being judged. Some of us feel listened to—but don't feel heard. That's usually because we believe the other person isn't being present while we are expressing ourselves. So sometimes we just quit . . . we just shut down. No more! The *Sacred Power of Your Ripple* invites you to shout your magnificence from every rooftop; to stop dimming your light and turn it up brighter; to say what's on your mind; to do what feels true in the moment; to risk failure; to express yourself from your heart; and to let your passion flow. You can express your voice through your physical appearance; through your job or your career; through your hobbies, interests, and causes; through your writings, posts, creations, and performances; and through the daily energy you flow into the world.

Expressing yourself physically, emotionally, and verbally is a very important aspect of the *Sacred Power of Your Ripple*. Each of us desperately needs to be heard in some way. Many of us feel the need to compel, convince, persuade, or convert others. Some of us just want what's inside of us to be witnessed by another. We are beings of expression and knowing someone is "listening" helps validate that we have meaning in this life.

LET YOUR VOICE BE HEARD!

Some of us express our ripple simply by putting ourselves out there. We want someone to know how we feel or what something means to us. We want people to see the "real" us at our best. We want someone to connect with us on our own terms. And, sometimes we simply need to share, release, vent, or commune. Whatever vehicle we choose, we can share and express ourselves in the form of encouragement, intimate encounters, and works of creativity. All are forms of the *Sacred Power of Your Ripple*—various expressions of letting your "voice" be heard. Choosing the right way to physically, emotionally, or tangibly purr or roar in the right moment makes all the difference. So stop playing small. Pick your moment. Let your voice be heard!

THREE SACRED GIFTS

The *Divine Principle of One* teaches that it actually is possible to infuse another person with new possibilities through the *Sacred Power of Your Ripple*. A powerful exercise for awakening this Sacred Power and flowing it into someone else is to *gift* them with three affirmations that remind them of their divine nature. We do this by transferring energy to them in the ripples of attention, affection, appreciation, and acceptance. These affirmations are referred to as *Sacred Gifts* and we can offer them in person, on the phone, in e-mail, text, or social media. The more direct and personal the exchange is, the greater the impact of the Sacred Gifts. Nothing is more powerful than gazing into a person's eyes and sharing a Sacred Gift. So I encourage you to invite a friend to share them back with you once you've flowed them out into the world.

My favorite Sacred Gifts are the following three sentences:

"You're beautiful!"
"You're doing a great job!"
"I love you!"

Stringing together these three simple phrases has the ability to ripple so deeply into someone else's consciousness that they will be shifted immediately and for hours. They will be impacted at such a deep level they will be inspired to share their experience with others, awakening the *Sacred Power of Their Own Ripple.* Sharing the Sacred Gifts can take any form you wish, but it's important that you are authentic with your sentiments. When we give a gift to someone, we don't nonchalantly toss it at them—we are transforming energy. The *Sacred Power of Your Ripple* teaches that we connect clearly with them at eye level and deeply with them at heart level, and then we lovingly, enthusiastically transfer the energy. That's the only way the Sacred Gift will have transformational power. The gift also needs to be consistent with the nature of the relationship. In most cases, telling an employee she is beautiful or that you love them can cross the line of appropriateness.

You and I have already traveled pretty far together. And since we don't have a work relationship, let me tell you right now: *You're beautiful! You're doing a great job! And I love you!* Let those words settle into you as you celebrate the *Sacred Power of Your Ripple.*

CHAPTER FIVE

THE SACRED POWER
OF SPIRIT

You look beyond the veil of form and separation.
This is the realization of oneness. This is love.

— Eckhart Tolle

Our spirituality is driven first by the *Sacred Power of Presence*. When we are fully present, we become aware of some divine force that is speaking to us in a timeless language. Perhaps you sense it coming from the outside world . . . a voice you hear or something that you see—some expression of nature like the stars in the night sky or the wind in the trees. Or maybe you are struck hearing someone laugh or say something you weren't expecting. You can sense it internally as well, as you contemplate or "feel" something inside. Sometimes it's very prominent in our awareness; other times it's just a faint whisper.

Whatever you interpret it to be, you know this presence is real. For thousands of years, the great sages, oracles, shamans, and philosophers referred to this essence outside of you and flowing through you as *Spirit*. Most wisdom traditions have described Spirit as immortal, invisible, and beyond our physical understanding. The ancient Indian text the Bhagavad Gita explains, "Weapons cannot cleave it. Fire cannot burn it, nor can water wet it, nor wind dry it. It is constant, capable of going everywhere, firm, immovable, and eternal."

Whether you apply a religious connotation to Spirit or see it through nondenominational eyes, we know that it is all-pervasive, flows through everything, and is infinite.

DEEPER STILL

The human brain can grasp some pretty complex concepts, but it is actually incapable of comprehending the true essence of infinity. We can understand it on a theoretical level, but fully appreciating the concept of an infinite, ever-expanding, and all-pervading Spirit is probably out of the question. We can, however, grasp the concept of a personal version of Spirit that rests inside us, which, throughout time, has been referred to as the *Soul*. And what is the Soul? It's the human expression of the Divine. It's our personal, individual expression of something much bigger than us—something way more expansive than we could ever really imagine.

It's not actually in our physical bodies. We just mistakenly think it is because our bodies are our reference points for all things. When we look in the mirror, we "think" we are looking at our self—but we are only gazing at the Soul's physical expression. If we peel away all the flesh, bones, muscles, organs, blood vessels, and tissues and go deeper still, until there is no physical aspect to our existence, our Soul is the essence beneath it all. When we say the word *I*, we often think we are talking about this physical flesh being that walks through the world, but what we really mean is my body, my mind, *and* my Soul. And when we leave this earthly existence, as we all must do at the end of our lives, our bodies return to dust, our minds move to a higher level of consciousness, and our Souls merge back into the divine one-ness of Spirit that is pure, unbounded, infinite, and ever present.

A Wave on the Ocean of Infinity

The Soul is simply our personal, individual expression of Spirit. When we look out at the ocean, we see it as a single object—a vast one-ness made up of an infinite number of water molecules. We don't see the ocean as separate pieces of water . . . we see it as one huge, never-ending entity extending to the horizon. To better understand the distinction between these two concepts, let's view the one-ness of the ocean as Spirit. But every few moments, a wave pops out of this one-ness of the ocean and individuates itself . . . separates itself from the whole. It rolls for a bit, cresting, frothing, and distinguishing itself from the vast blueness beneath it. It develops its own "personality." Then, at a certain point, when the individualized wave has exhausted itself on its journey of separation, it collapses back into the infinite one-ness of the ocean, merging with every other droplet of water that makes up the whole. If the ocean can be seen as Spirit, then the wave is the Soul . . . separating itself from the one-ness of the whole for the span of its lifetime—and then at a certain point collapsing back into the divine flow.

I have a Soul and you have a Soul and every living being on the planet has a Soul. That is why we are all so connected. Each of us is an individuated expression of the *Divine Principle of One*. And the *Sacred Power of Spirit* reminds us in every moment that we are merely one breath, one blink, one heartbeat away from merging back into the one-ness of the eternal, timeless cosmic flow.

The *Sacred Power of Spirit* operates on three levels of awareness:

1. Our awareness of the one-ness of the divine Spirit, which contains everything in existence—including our own essence.

2. Our awareness that *our own Soul* is an individuated and personal expression of that divine Spirit.

3. Our awareness of our deep connection to *everyone else's Soul* because they are also individuated and personal expressions of the divine Spirit.

Throughout time, these three levels of awareness have been referred to as levels of consciousness. The term *consciousness* is discussed a lot in spiritual circles, and it can easily be defined as the expanded self-awareness of our own Soul, the Souls of others, and the divine Spirit, which runs through everything.

YOUR OWN SOUL

We were born mortal, human, flawed, and imperfect in so many ways. We say things we wish we hadn't; we do things we wish we could take back; we stumble; we fall; we make poor decisions; we move in wrong directions; we think dark thoughts; and we are sometimes filled with regret. And then there is the best version of ourself—brilliant in every moment. As we walk these Five Divine Paths and awaken our Sacred Powers, we begin to fully align with the Universe, and with the support of Spirit, we then evolve into our best versions.

We've all had times when we've done the perfect thing at the exact right moment, summoned the most brilliant words at the ideal time, and "magically" came up with the solution to an impossible problem. But that's not how we express ourselves most of the time. Yet we know we can. We know that somewhere deep within us rests our best version, just waiting to spring forth. Spirituality is the journey each of us takes in every moment, to channel the Universe and flow its magnificence through our individuated Soul and connect to our best version—if only for a moment.

THE SOULS OF OTHERS

There have been times in our life when we have felt deeply linked to another person. We have felt a profound bond, a sense of connection that transcends the physical realm. It's deeper than friendship and more expansive than sexual attraction. It's an awakening that we've either known the other person in another life or have somehow spent much more time with them in this life than we actually have. This feeling of deep familiarity is an expression of the *Divine Principle of One*, which makes us aware of something inside of them that's also in us—a sort of Universal recognition of divine energy. There are many interpretations of this sense of union, but the most popular term is *soul mate.*

Sensing this soul connection doesn't necessarily mean you have found your mate for life. But it does mean that you sense the same kindred Spirit in them that is flowing in your own Soul. Spirit is everywhere, just like the one-ness of the ocean. And our Souls are like the waves that separate from that one-ness of the ocean to express their unique individuality. It's as if one wave in the ocean says to another wave, "OMG. You're part of this vast essence also? Me too!" So, in the deepest sense, when you become aware of someone else's Soul, *you see the same ocean in their wave that's in your wave.* It's a magnificent feeling. And as our awareness ebbs and flows, so can our ability to sense the same Spirit in their Soul that's in our Soul.

The Sanskrit greeting *Namaste* literally means "I bow to you." But the more modern interpretation is, "I honor the divine light in you that's also in me. And when you're in that space, and I'm in that space, we are one." This is what's going on at a very deep level when we sense our soul mate. When we awaken the *Sacred Power of Spirit* in our life, our Soul expands, and our own inner light starts to shine more brightly. And as we move through the world, we become more aware of this divine light in others. Soon we start experiencing soul mates all around us (which is why you shouldn't jump into marriage with the first soul mate you meet!).

MERGING WITH THE DIVINE SPIRIT

Consciousness of our own Soul and the Souls of others is how we crystallize our true connection with divine Spirit. The more we open to the sensations of our own Soul, the deeper our understanding goes. Our personal Soul is essentially a channel—the translation device for Spirit, which is so vast, so infinite, so beyond our comprehension, that without "that light shining within you," a state of true one-ness could never be experienced. Your Soul understands the pure one-ness of divine Spirit, speaks its language, and is connected to it in every moment. But it is our awareness of our Soul that allows us to feel this sacred connection.

NONDUALISM AND THE SACRED POWER OF SPIRIT

Many of the ageless spiritual teachings are based on the concept of the *Divine Principle of One*—the belief that there is no separation between anything. The ancient spiritual masters referred to this one-ness as *Advaita* (pronounced ad-vite-ah), literally translated as "nondualism." Advaita teaches that we are multidimensional beings and that all the various aspects of our existence are simply Spirit wearing different disguises. The core of this ancient teaching of nondualism states that there is:

- No difference between your physical body and your personal Soul

- No distinction between your personal Soul and the Soul of another

- No separation between your personal Soul and the Universal Spirit

If we peel away the artificial illusions of separation, known in Sanskrit as *maya*, then our one-ness is revealed. Spirituality is simply our relationship to the Universe, a way of seeing the world in which we are simultaneously different parts of the whole as well as the whole. And it is from our Soul that we flow so effortlessly into Spirit and merge with the divine.

SOUL AWAKENING

The easiest and yet most powerful way for us to awaken our Soul is by connecting to the calm, unblemished, quietude that rests within. But our earthbound world has become pretty noisy. It clamors for our attention from the moment we wake up until the moment we close our eyes to sleep. But the stillness and silence of our Soul that rests deep within is the most tranquil place we could ever spend our time. It is the land of serenity, beyond space and time, beyond thoughts and physical sensations, beyond fears of the future and memories of the past. It is pure, whole, and perfect—uncorrupted by pain, sadness, and regret. It is the primary gift that the *Sacred Power of Spirit* has bestowed upon us.

It is the eternal reminder that we are holy and sacred, that even though we are flesh-bound, earth-bound, flawed, and mortal, we have been birthed from something so magnificent, glorious, and powerful that it defies words.

The Soul Awakening Meditation

We can begin your Soul awakening right now with the Soul Awakening Meditation. Find a place where you can sit or lie down, and get as comfortable as possible.

Through your nose, take a long, slow, deep breath in, and watch the breath as it moves into you and goes down deep into your belly. Release the breath, and observe it as it moves up your chest and back out through your nose. Continue to witness as you slowly breathe in and breathe out five times. Patiently watch your breathing and notice that you are starting to slow down.

As you continue to breathe, now place your hand on the space where you feel the breath entering you. This doesn't have to be your heart. You may feel the breath entering you through the top of your head or your forehead, nose, mouth, throat, solar plexus, or belly . . . even your ears. Place your hand on that space, and just connect to your breath through this physical location. Take a big, deep breath in through your nostrils to help you find that spot.

As you breathe in, feel your breath enter you, moving past your fingers, and then move your attention to the space you've identified. And, gently, let the breath leave you through that same space. You are awakening the Soul.

As you breathe, feel free to adjust your fingers up, down, right, or left to connect more closely with the exact space where your breath is coming into you. And throughout the meditation, if you suddenly feel that the location has changed, move your fingers there. Continue to breathe. Feel the breath move past your fingertips. Now allow your eyes to slowly close, continue the process, and see if you can stay in this space for five minutes.

I'm guessing you're back now. What was it like to fully surrender to the divine flow of the Universe? What was it like to visit the stillness and silence in your Soul? What was it like to awaken it? What was it like to commune with Spirit?

Write your answers down on the Soul Awakening Experience sheet below. Don't filter or censor your experiences—just write. Feel free to add your insights on a daily basis as you continue to connect to the Divine with a daily practice.

My Soul Awakening Experiences

1. _____

   _____

   _____

2. _____

   _____

   _____

3. _____

   _____

   _____

4. _____

   _____

   _____

5. _____

   _____

   _____

6. _____

_____

_____

7. _____

_____

_____

8. _____

_____

_____

9. _____

_____

_____

10. _____

_____

_____

SUBTLE BENEFITS OF DIVINE AWAKENING

Each time you practice the Soul Awakening Meditation, a deeper experience will occur. Sometimes you will feel the impact immediately, and you'll carry it with you in a more overt way. Other times the effects will be more subtle. No matter what you feel right after the meditation, know in your core that you have awakened your Soul and made a deep communion with Spirit. The Divine is flowing through every thought you have, every word you speak, every action you take, and every decision you make.

Modern science has proven the vast physical and emotional benefits of a regular practice of presence, from a heightened immune system to lower blood pressure to more restful sleep. But the ancient sages who awakened and mastered the *Sacred Power of Spirit* revealed even more profound discoveries that most modern scientists are still resisting. You and I are the legacy of those findings. We know that by applying the *Divine Principle of One* to our lives, even greater benefits will flow to us in every moment. As everything in our twirling world slows down—just a little—we become calmer, have greater clarity, and are more patient and compassionate. Stress and anxiety drift away. We listen better and start to make more thoughtful choices, and happiness pursues us. Oh, and we actually get to merge with the Divine!

The timeless wisdom contained in the *Divine Principle of One* is ours for the asking. Awakening our *Sacred Power of Presence* will allow us to flow through the world with greater grace and greater ease. Once our ability to seize the present moment has been cultivated, the *Sacred Power of Your Ripple* will awaken a more profound connection to all beings, creating deeper meaning in your life. Through the *Sacred Power of Spirit*, the essence of who you are—your very *Soul*—will awaken, sparking miracles in every moment, infusing your dreams and desires with higher purpose.

CHAPTER SIX

LIVING THE DIVINE PRINCIPLE OF ONE

Once you make a decision,
the universe conspires to make it happen.

— Joseph Campbell

THE DAILY PRACTICES

You can awaken the *Divine Principle of One* in your life and the *Sacred Powers of Presence, Your Ripple, and Spirit* through five powerful daily practices that can be used individually or in combination. Each practice offers you an opportunity to cultivate your ability to connect with the present moment and merge with the Divine throughout the day. All five practiced on a daily basis will transform you dramatically, shifting your life forever in ways you never dreamed, as you become as infinite as the Universe. These Sacred Rituals are the following five daily practices:

1. The *Five Sacred Questions* to Awaken Presence
2. The Soul Awakening Meditation
3. The Sacred Affirmation for the *Divine Principle of One*
4. The Sacred Mantra of the *Divine Principle of One*
5. The Sacred Rite for Awakening *Your Ripple*

THE FIVE SACRED QUESTIONS TO AWAKEN PRESENCE

We start our day by asking the *Five Sacred Questions* to expand your ability to shift your awareness out of the past, away from the future, and into this sacred, precious present moment. Find a quiet place to sit or lie down, and begin the process by asking the following questions:

1. Do I agree I cannot step into the past and change it?

2. Do I agree I cannot step into the future to force it?

3. Do I have the patience to wait until my mud settles and the water is clear?

4. Do I give myself permission to show up right now as my best, most brilliant, most creative expression of myself?

5. Am I willing to breathe deeply into this moment and awaken my best version?

With your eyes closed, and your hand on your heart, simply ask each question once and reply with either a yes or no. If you have answered no, go back to the question and ask it again. If it is still no, move on to practicing the Soul Awakening Meditation, and then try again.

Sometimes answers will flow, and sometimes there will be no answers. The key is to be honest with yourself and see your constrictions for what they are. You know deep inside that when you are at your best, you answer all the Sacred Questions with a yes. When you get to the point where you consistently answer these five questions with a yes, you are able to live in the present moment. The rest will take care of itself as you awaken your Sacred Powers.

PRACTICING THE SOUL AWAKENING MEDITATION

Find a restful place where you can sit or lie down. Get as comfortable as possible, and surrender to the Soul Awakening Meditation we just practiced in the previous chapter. Remember, comfort is queen. So keep moving toward comfort. And feel free to sit each day for at least five minutes and as long as thirty minutes. Once you have mastered this meditation, you can even introduce a mantra or weave an affirmation into your practice.

THE SACRED AFFIRMATION
FOR THE DIVINE PRINCIPLE OF ONE

Affirmations are powerful expressions that embed into our consciousness to shift our thinking. We explore these more deeply in Chapter 7 as we learn to plant intentions and manifest our dreams as we walk the Divine Path of Awareness. *The Sacred Affirmation for the Divine Principle of One* will set the trajectory for our continued awakening. This ancient Sanskrit vibration has been uttered for thousands of years to shift the mind-set from the personal to the Universal. Repeating it out loud upon waking up, and then throughout the day whenever you feel tired, weak, constricted, or stuck, will snap you out of feeling small and remind you of your true divine connection to the Universe.

Aham brahmasmi—I am the UNIVERSE.

We pronounce this ancient vibration just as it's spelled. And for more than 5,000 years, millions of enlightened beings have used it to invoke their own divine connection to Source. This vibration has been whispered and chanted so many times throughout the millennia that it is firmly etched into the cosmic flow. When you repeat it, you join yourself to that eternal energy.

THE SACRED MANTRA FOR THE DIVINE PRINCIPLE OF ONE

The Sacred Mantra to remind you of the one-ness between your Soul and the Universal Spirit is:

AYAM ATMA BRAHMAN

This is one of the oldest mantras in existence. It comes from an ancient Indian teaching known in Sanskrit as the *Maha Vakyas*. *Maha* means "master" or "great"; *Vakya* is "saying." This mantra is one of the *Great Sayings* and it means *my personal soul is merged with the Universal Spirit*. Throughout the day or in moments of feeling that you are not woven into the magnificence of Divine Spirit, just whisper, *"ayam atma brahman,"* and your Soul will reconnect itself to the cosmic flow of all existence.

Each day that you practice the *Sacred Rituals of the Divine Principle of One*, you will merge more effortlessly with the Divine. You will become more present in all your interactions. As you move throughout your day, you will notice the transformational impact of your ripple. Your Soul will awaken, and you will begin cultivating a deeper relationship with the eternal Spirit. In time, you will become a living, breathing expression of the *Divine Principle of One*.

THE SACRED RITE FOR AWAKENING *YOUR RIPPLE*

As you begin your day, stand up, feet shoulder-width apart. Start off by placing your palms together, and bring them to your heart. Now slowly extend your right arm out to the side, cup the air, and bring it back to your heart. Then extend your left arm out to the side, cup the air, and bring it back to your heart. Continue the movement, bending your knees a bit, as you alternate the movement with both arms. Relax your body, and begin to reach farther in each direction, bringing the energy of the Universe into your heart. Develop a rhythm, and turn it into a dance by swaying your body as you lean into each direction, until you have created a constant flow. Feel free to put on some music that will allow you to be less rigid, and relax your body. And then close your eyes as you feel the Universe flow into you with each movement and as the Sacred Power of Your Ripple flows into every expression of your Being. As you dance, silently repeat the Sacred Affirmation:

Aham brahmasmi—I am the Universe

It's often been said that if you really want to learn something deeply, learn to teach it. But the reality is that before we can ever share with others, we need to authentically practice the teachings we wish to learn. The most direct way to embed any concept into our heart is to live it. Practicing these daily rituals with some level of consistency will awaken the teachings within you at the level of the Soul. In just a few days, the *Divine Principle of One* will ripple through every cell in your body. Remember: ritual + meaning = transformation!

The Second Secret

THE
DIVINE PRINCIPLE
OF AWARENESS

The Divine Principle of Awareness
and
the Sacred Powers of
Attention . . . Intention . . . and Action

CHAPTER SEVEN

WALKING THE SECOND DIVINE PATH

At the Intersection of Dream and Possibility

*The Master acts without doing anything
and teaches without saying anything.
Things arise and she lets them come;
things disappear and she lets them go.
She has but doesn't possess,
acts but doesn't expect.
When her work is done, she forgets it.
That is why it lasts forever.*

— Lao-tzu

I AM THE MASTER OF THIS MOMENT

Every moment in our existence begins with awareness. If we are not aware of something, it doesn't exist in our consciousness. But when we place our attention on that thing . . . *poof!* It becomes "real." Now that you have awakened your Soul, the *Divine Principle of Awareness* is the evolutionary starting point for transforming the world around you as you transform yourself! It's the cornerstone for every step you take to move your life from where it is to where you'd like to be. Establishing ourselves in a state of expanded awareness raises our vibration and suddenly places us in a position to make better decisions—choices driven by courage, strength, our best version, and our highest truth rather than from a space of fear, desperation, or weakness. This new, empowered mind-set gives us the spark to continue our spiritual journey and navigate with confidence, clarity, and deeper understanding.

Think back to when you woke up this morning. Prior to the millisecond that you drifted from your final wave of sleep into a waking state, nothing was "real." Maybe you remember the last few seconds of your dream. Or maybe you were totally unconscious. But then, for some reason—maybe your alarm rang, the sun rose, the dog barked, or the garbage truck made that grinding sound—you became *conscious*. One of the hallmarks of being in an awake or conscious state is that as we absorb the world through our five senses, *we become aware* of what we are hearing, seeing, tasting, smelling, thinking, and, ultimately, of what we are feeling.

Depending on the depth of that awareness, we then unfold a progression of neurological, electrical, chemical, and physical interactions that move us to *focus our attention* onto something; then to *set an intention* regarding that *object of our attention*; and then to *take action* in order to achieve our goal. This conscious choice-making process can be as simple as opening your eyes to look at the clock, wanting to turn off the alarm, and then tapping the snooze button, or realizing you have an early morning meeting, desiring to get out of the house quickly, and then jumping out of bed. And, throughout our day, the process can be as complex as becoming aware that your current job, relationship, or circumstance is no longer serving you; then deciding to shift that narrative; and then physically leaving that situation! Everything starts with awareness, then flows to a state of desire, and then unfolds into an action. Everything. Even if you should decide that your action is to take no action!

We understand the modern science behind this sequence now, but 2,500 years ago, the basics of this process were inscribed in an ancient Indian holy book—the Bhagavad Gita—with the Sanskrit words: *yogastha kuru karmani*. Translated into English, it provides the fundamental guidance embedded in the Second Divine Principle—essentially to *establish yourself first in the present moment, and then perform action.*

The *Divine Principle of Awareness* has existed for eternity. And there are three Sacred Powers that have upheld this timeless truth of transformation since mankind and womankind first walked the earth. Awakening them heightens your awareness, aligns you more closely with the Universe, sets your world in motion, and begins the process of manifestation. These three progressive Sacred Powers are:

- The Sacred Power of Attention
- The Sacred Power of Intention
- The Sacred Power of Action

Activating these three Sacred Powers is critical for an evolutionary shift to occur *in your life*. And once they are activated *as the starting point for how you see the world*, transformation flows effortlessly. It's pretty simple. And, it starts by engraining these three self-reflections into your awareness:

- Where is my attention in a given moment?
- What is the intention I'm bringing to that moment?
- What action will flow from my intention?

Attention is the activator of intention, intention is the spark of transformation, and action converts the energy flow into your tangible reality.

CHAPTER EIGHT

THE SACRED POWER OF ATTENTION

*The moment one gives close attention to any thing,
even a blade of grass, it becomes a mysterious, awesome,
indescribably magnificent world in itself.*

— Henry Miller

The power of attention is the doorway to our ultimate transformation.
Without it, we are sleepwalking through life. By recognizing it,
harnessing it, and cultivating it, we truly become the master of
each moment! Awakening our awareness is the starting point for
every step we will take from this moment forward. It's the foundational element of making conscious choices. It's the key to living
life with our eyes wide-open. And when we see the world from an
expansive, totally aware perspective, clarity will unfold. A sense of
empowerment will guide our thoughts, we will make better decisions, and fulfillment will begin to bubble up from deep within.

Transformation is simply not possible without *Attention, Intention,* and *Action.* You've heard the saying, "Where attention goes
energy flows." A perfect example would be right now. As you read
these words, they are absorbing your full attention. Everything
else in your life has drifted into the background. But if we drift our
attention to what you ate for dinner last night, then you are there.

Drift your attention to your childhood. To your astrological sign. To your mother. To your clothes. See how far you've drifted away from last night's dinner? Now go back just one more day, one more dinner that has probably faded from your memory a bit as well. Over the past 48 hours, as your attention was consumed by other things, that dinner from only two days ago has no longer stayed fresh in your mind's eye.

Whatever you place your attention on will grow and blossom and bloom; and whatever you drift it away from will wither and diminish and die. There are many definitions that we can apply to the concept of attention. Is it a concentrated focus? Being present in the moment? Or simply general awareness?

The easiest way to understand this timeless principle is in our own lives. Let's start with our daily to-do list. Each day we wake up with a vague group of things we want to accomplish. Write something, communicate with someone, buy something, go somewhere, work on a project. Of course this is in addition to all the things we already have going on. By the time we've finished our morning meditation, the list is a swirl of 100 items.

The moment we drift our focus to one item in that swirl, 99 others drift into the background. That is the power of attention. As we delve deeper into that one item or issue, it takes on a greater power. We can analyze it, assess it, deconstruct it, alter it, break it down, or build it up, but each millisecond we spend on this one item clears the slate of all the other issues that were critical moments before.

THE OBJECT OF YOUR ATTENTION

Whatever you focus your attention on becomes "the object of your attention." This could be as simple as staring at a TV screen, reading a blog, or watching a video. And it can include broad categories such as family issues, health concerns, matters of the heart, business challenges, financial issues, even our spiritual practice. In fact, this is the key to mindfulness and meditation!

In every style of meditation, there is an object of your attention. We watch our breath, gaze at something, or silently repeat a sacred word, mantra, or vibration. When we notice we've drifted away to thoughts, sounds, or physical sensations, we simply drift back. Plainly put, mastering meditation is cultivating our ability to gently drift back to that object of our attention regardless of the waterfall of thoughts that may cascade down upon us. And as we continuously cultivate this skill, ultimately, our full attention more easily arrives at the present moment and in that moment, all other activity vanishes.

Following your breath in and out is an easy "object of your attention." So rather than just reading about it, let's experience it together.

Gently breathe in and out through your nostrils, and direct your attention to your breath. You've been breathing all along, but now you have your attention on it. Keep breathing. And keep watching your breath. You'll witness your breath as you inhale, and you'll witness your breath as you exhale. Don't hold it in or out, and don't feel the need to count. Simply keep breathing naturally in a relaxed way. Feel your body relax. Inhale and watch your chest rise. Then gently exhale and watch it settle back down. Rising and falling. Keep observing. Keep watching. Keep witnessing the movement of your breath. Feel it in your nose. Feel it in your chest. Feel it as it comes in. Feel it as it leaves you.

As you continue this gentle witnessing process, you'll feel yourself starting to slow down. But as you proceed, you will also notice that your attention expands and drifts to thoughts, sounds, or other physical sensations. This is totally normal. But isn't it interesting, that within seconds, your attention has drifted away from the initial object of your attention to a new one?

During any meditation or mindfulness exercise, when you notice that you've drifted away, simply drift your attention back to your breath. Since you're using your breath as the object of your attention, no matter where you drift, you come back to the breath. Keep coming back to the breath . . . back to the breath.

Now try it with your eyes closed, and just breathe and witness, watch, observe. There's nothing else to do other than watch the in and out of your breathing. This is mindfulness.

Let's practice it for a few minutes right now. Take your time. I'll wait. Close your eyes and begin.

Welcome back. Congratulations! You've just meditated using your breath as the object of your attention. The next time you hear the words *mindful* or *mindfulness*, you will know exactly what they mean. You are now a mindfulness meditator!

We can follow our breath to meditate, or we can use another technique called mantra meditation. When we meditate on a mantra, we place our attention not on our breath but on a word or phrase. In the ancient Indian language of Sanskrit, that word or phrase is called a mantra, which comes from two Sanskrit words: *man*, meaning "mind," and *tra*, meaning "vehicle." So a mantra is essentially a mind vehicle. No matter where our mind drifts, as long as we have an object of our attention (such as our breath or a mantra), we will stay present.

The key to attention rests in the here and now. Because in the present moment, everything is fresh, rich, larger than life, and most important—*actionable*. The past contains only memories, and there's nothing we can really do about them. We can't go back in time and change the words we said or the action we took. The past is carved in stone, and that's why beating ourselves up over what's already been done makes no sense. We can't unring the bell. But we can take steps in the present moment to carve new stones and make a better choice!

The future has yet to unfold. It's a projection, a dream that may or may not come true. And that's why fearing what we believe *might* happen is also a waste of time and energy. Most often, what we fear is usually far worse than what actually unfolds. We can place our intentions into the future, but the only action that can impact the future is the one we take right here, right now, in the present moment.

So we have a choice in every given moment about where we want to place our attention: the past, the present, or the future. And if we are looking to shift our life from where we are to where we'd like to be, it seems like folly to be anywhere but in that sacred, precious present moment since that is the only moment we can actually influence.

WHERE'S YOUR ATTENTION?

Think of everything else in your life that you've drifted your attention to over the past few days. How about that conversation you recently had with a close friend of yours? Maybe you've been obsessing over what someone else is thinking. How about the internal conversations you've been having with yourself about your health, your aging, your love life, your relatives, your money? What aspects of those issues has your attention been focused on? Successes or failures? Satisfaction or fear? Self-reflection or rumination? And how much has your attention been on these issues? Let's cut to the core right now and explore your current state of attention.

In the space below, write down the three biggest challenges, fears, or concerns that have been consuming your attention over the past few days. Next to each issue, write down what you perceive as the most likely outcome of each situation:

Where My Attention Is Right Now

	Issue	Expected Outcome
1.	_____	_____
2.	_____	_____
3.	_____	_____

It all comes down to attention. Wherever your attention is, you're giving power and energy—consciously or unconsciously—to the outcome you anticipate. If you fear the outcome, it prevents your natural ability of intention to unfold. If you are working toward the outcome, you are in the process of manifesting the outcome. When we expand our thinking and allow more possibilities to enter into our awareness—even just a little bit—our *Sacred Power of Attention* will begin to provide solutions.

So now write down the same three biggest challenges, fears, or concerns that have been consuming your attention over the past few days. Except this time, instead of writing down the most likely outcome, write down what you believe to be the best possible outcome—the one that would be a great solution to the challenge, transcend your fear, ease your concerns, or replace any anxiety you have with relief, satisfaction, and happiness.

	Issue	Best Possible Outcome
1.	_____	_____
2.	_____	_____
3.	_____	_____

Using the *Power of Attention* is like shining a flashlight in the darkness. Wherever we point its beam instantly becomes the reality of the moment. Do you notice the difference in how you feel when your attention is on the best possible outcome rather than a feared outcome?

The skeptic in you might say, "Well, of course I feel better when I think about the best thing that could happen." But that's the whole purpose of this process, to help you realize that it's always a choice of where we want to place our attention. Sometimes when we get so familiar with the possibility of a negative outcome, we start expecting it, believing that it's the *only* outcome—and it becomes a self-fulfilling prophecy. But outcomes are in the future, and the future is never carved in stone. At best it's a guess of what we believe is likely to unfold.

Let's do the exercise just one more time, but this time, next to your three biggest challenges, fears, or concerns that have been consuming your attention over the past few days, write down a third possible outcome. Not your most likely outcome, or the best possible one, but an outcome that could unfold that you'd never thought of before.

	Issue	My Third Possible Outcome
1.	_____	_____
2.	_____	_____
3.	_____	_____

Now you have three different outcomes for each pressing issue: *the expected outcome, your best possible outcome,* and *your third possible outcome.* As you reflect on each issue, there even may be additional outcomes that have come to mind. Now place your hand on your heart, and for each issue, ask yourself, "Which outcome do I truly desire?" Not "Which one do I expect?" but "Which outcome does my heart truly long for?" As the answers flow, write the desired outcomes below:

My Desired Outcomes

1. _____
2. _____
3. _____

This is a pretty simple, yet fairly powerful process. It can be intense to look at your life and start moving it in the direction of your dreams. But where you once were stuck or resigned to a particular outcome, you can now see other possibilities. Remember: we have very little control over the outcomes that unfold in our life. We can influence them, spark them, and direct them, but in the end the Universe decides. We do, however, *have total control over our outlook.* And what we have just done through this exercise is expand our outlook! This is hard work. But you are cultivating your awareness at a very high level, and this is where intention comes into play.

CHAPTER NINE

THE SACRED POWER
OF INTENTION

*Don't judge each day by the harvest you reap
but by the seeds that you plant.*

— Robert Louis Stevenson

Intention is a transformational law of nature; it's the seed that already holds within it the fulfillment of your dream. It is the unfolding of your vision waiting to be birthed. Your intention is a seed, like any other seed—the seed of a blade of grass, a zucchini flower, an avocado tree, the acorn that contains the whole oak tree in its one little inch of intention. If they are not planted, not nourished, and not watered, seeds can stay in their seed form forever. The ground can be littered with acorns, and no oak will grow from them. But a little bit of fertile soil, a little bit of rain, a little bit of light, and the right climate . . . and suddenly you have the beginnings of a mighty tree. While attention is a present-moment activity, your intention is always for the future.

An intention is a desire of yours that has gone through your intellect and *been selected as something you will place more of your attention on.* Think of your intellect as a giant filter through which every thought, sound, and physical sensation passes. We ignore most of them because there are so many, and most are not critical

67

in the moment. Our attention is elsewhere, and so they slip right by. For example, right now as you read this, there may be noise around you. Maybe a plane is passing overhead or a voice is speaking far away. Maybe a dog is barking. Perhaps you even notice the sound of your breath. But if your attention was right here with me, most likely you haven't heard a sound.

THE PATH FROM ATTENTION TO INTENTION

Obviously your inner ear heard it, interpreted the vibration, and even processed it. But because your attention wasn't on it, that sound drifted right past your awareness. Maybe now that your attention is on it, it's become louder or more relevant to you. So think about this for a moment: 70,000 thoughts a day are pouring into your mind, sounds are constantly tickling the tiny bones in your inner ear, nonstop physical sensations are rippling through every part of your body. But you only notice them when you choose to place your attention on them. Yes, attention is a choice!

ATTENTION LEADS TO INTENTION

Once we direct our *attention at* or *on* something, the powerful process of *intention* begins. That's right—even though *intention* is a noun and not a verb, it's actually a process. Here's how it works: the moment our attention falls on something, we instantly begin *the process* of mentally digesting the experience through a lightning-fast processor we refer to as our *intellect*. It evaluates each moment through an internal filtration system that you apply to everything. In his novel *Still Life with Woodpecker*, the author Tom Robbins refers to this process as the choice between "yum" or "yuk." We unconsciously judge every thought, sound, image, sensation, word of a conversation, and moment in time as serving us or not serving us, positive or negative, comfortable or uncomfortable, valuable or irrelevant, producing pain or soothing it. And each of us has a lifetime of personal experience that unconsciously determines how we will translate the object of our attention into the next moment.

TRANSFORMING DESIRES INTO INTENTIONS

Once we judge something as comfort creating or discomfort creating, we can decide to do something with it—essentially choose to allow or reject it, embrace or resist it, receive more or get less of it, or continue or stop. Right now our body and mind are filled with thousands of desires. The desire to feel more comfortable; the desire to scratch an itch; the desire to make peace with someone; the desire to read the next sentence; the desire to be happy; the desire to reflect on a painful moment; the desire to take a deep breath. Thousands of desires fall by the wayside as they pass through this yum-yuk filtering process; but if we cultivate them, they become intentions.

WHAT AM I AIMING AT?

It's easy to get confused over setting an intention. Should it be big? Or small? Attainable? Or beyond reach? Should it be about me or another person? But if the definition of *intention* is simply to have in mind a purpose or plan to direct the mind—*to aim*—then there is no right or wrong way to approach it. We get to choose every aspect of our intention! That's right. In every moment, we get to determine where we place our attention, and then, most important, what we will do with it.

The *Divine Principle of Awareness* encourages us to simply pay attention to whatever we desire, holding a magnifying glass on the object of our attention. We could wish health for someone else. As long as our attention stays on that intention, we will start to make physical, real-world choices to help them heal. Maybe we end up calling them, writing them, visiting them, rooting for them, or nourishing them in some way. Maybe your intention is for more love in your life. Then as long as your attention stays rooted in this vision, your actions will soon follow. With unwavering attention, a clear intention, and continued patience, your inner dialogue will ultimately become your outer dialogue, and your life will flow in the direction of your vision. If what you truly seek is more love, then you'll start taking certain actions, such as being kinder to yourself, making self-care a priority, forgiving yourself for past mistakes, opening your heart to let some more love in, and so on. And as long as you continue to shine the spotlight of attention onto the thing you truly seek, the intention will be nourished. Remember, an intention is simply *directing the mind toward a purpose or plan.* So as long as you are aiming and continue to aim without being distracted by all the other shiny objects around you, your intention will manifest.

SINGLE-POINTED INTENTION

The *Divine Principle of Awareness* teaches us to aim at one target at a time. A common misunderstanding regarding intention setting is that the more targets we can aim at, the higher the likelihood that our arrow will hit the mark. This couldn't be further from the truth. If we are looking for real transformation, we need to embrace the concept of *single-pointedness of intention.* If your seed is right about to nestle into the stillness of your heart and soul, and you interrupt that process by bringing in another seed, and then another, and then another, the stillness vanishes in the swirl of activity. Your nourishing becomes diluted, the garden becomes crowded, and most likely, the seed will not grow. That is the power of single-pointed intention. If we are truly going to manifest transformation in our life, we should focus on only one intention at a time—one seed . . . one garden . . . one moment—all leading up to effortless growth. That's why patience is so critical to the process of manifesting. Seeds take time to grow—and they require nourishment—and if your attention is off planting other seeds, then the original one you planted will wither from neglect.

INCREASING THE ODDS
THAT MY INTENTION WILL MANIFEST

Remember: You and I are earthbound, time-bound personal expressions of the Divine—individual unfoldings of the magnificent, infinite Universe, which is eternal—never born and never died. So, realistically, our most perfect intention should be to flow the Divine with every thought, breath, word, and action. But being sealed in this human body for the span of a lifetime makes it more challenging, confusing, and complicated. We get caught up in our humanness. We often think small, trying to make stuff happen in a given moment because we mistakenly believe it will bring us happiness or fulfillment. We set our sights on finding the perfect partner when we don't even love ourselves unconditionally. We desire the wealth we observe around us, when we ourselves don't fully practice abundance consciousness. We try so hard to make other people shift their beliefs, when we aren't fully conscious of our own.

The world around us is moving at light speed, and most of us are just trying to hold on, keep up, and do our best. And this is why the *Five Divine Principles* have not been embraced more broadly in our world. Most people are simply too distracted by life's twists and turns to place their attention on what really matters to them. Once you adopt these teachings as your framework, you begin to truly live every moment with deeper fulfillment. You begin to make conscious choices to help you get out of your own way, let go of self-doubt, release limiting beliefs, and allow your self-created barriers to fall away. From that place of understanding, you can easily channel whatever you were meant to flow. It's really that simple.

Our intentions can be as tiny as taking a deep breath in the midst of a challenging moment and as big as surrendering to the divine plan of the Universe. There's no right or wrong. We get to choose. But whatever intention we decide on can be fueled only by action.

CHAPTER TEN

THE SACRED POWER
OF ACTION

Do you want to know who you are?
Don't ask. Act! Action will delineate and define you.

— Thomas Jefferson

ACTIVATING OUR INTENTIONS

Once a desire goes through the transformational process of becoming an intention, it gets massaged one more time to determine the right moment to be acted on. Intentions that are not acted on drift into the background, wither away, and are replaced by new intentions that you've given a higher priority. The more attention you place on an intention, the more it grows. And the moment you choose to act on it—moving it from thought, concept, or idea into real-world, tangible reality—a flow of energy has been put in motion. Action leads to change, and change leads to growth. And growth is where you are headed!

The timeless principle that *energy cannot be created or destroyed; it can only be transformed* applies to your intentions as well. Once we move an intention from our minds into the physical world, it becomes activated. The energy that was infused in that thought is now transformed into the tangible world—taking on a life of its own. So simply saying your intention *out loud* creates a new ripple of energy. And we can activate an intention in many other ways, such as:

- Write it down, type it up, or journal about it.
- Share it online with others by blogging, tweeting, chatting, or posting it.
- Directly share it with another person—by phone, message, or a face-to-face conversation.
- Perform a physical action that reinforces the intention and sets it in motion.

Once you have taken the powerful step to move the intention from the silence of your heart out into the world, it becomes a sacred agreement between your personal self and your Universal Self, the highest version of who you are.

What I seek, I already am.

THE DIVINE CONSPIRACY

Intentions don't simply create a ripple of energy. Once activated, they have the unique ability to coordinate and merge all the moving parts needed for their actualization. In a magnificent *divine conspiracy*, they build on themselves, growing, expanding, and collecting all the missing pieces, people, and circumstances necessary for their ultimate fulfillment. But they require constant cultivation in the form of attention to keep this divine conspiracy unfolding.

In his timeless classic *Walden*, Henry David Thoreau wrote, "We loiter in winter while it is already spring," and what a perfect metaphor for the *Divine Principle of Awareness*. If one foot is mired in the quicksand of old blockages, tired excuses, stale philosophies, and constricted ways of seeing the world, then how can our next step be the strong one that pulls us out of the quicksand and launches us in the direction of our dreams? Only through activating the *Sacred Powers of Attention, Intention*, and then *Action* can we truly transform.

Dreams are also dormant, waiting to be fertilized, and that fertilization mechanism is action. And when you're able to merge attention, intention, and action, the divine conspiracy will awaken. Transformation is sparked by attention, which births the seed of intention. And then a second dose of attention is necessary to move the intention into the physical world, where it can actualize and sprout.

So what do you want more of in your life? Less of? And what step can you take today to activate the fulfillment of your intentions?

In the spaces below, write down your top three intentions. Next to each one, write down the activation step you will take to begin the flow of energy into the physical world. Remember, your action step can be as simple as writing your intention on a Post-it note, sending an e-mail, preparing to have a difficult conversation, or volunteering for a cause that sparks your passion.

Activating My Top Intentions

My Intention	Real World Activation Step
1. _____	_____
2. _____	_____
3. _____	_____

So many intentions never materialize because we hold them tightly trapped in our mind. They get diminished in the swirl of all the other things we're trying to keep straight in our brains. If you haven't yet written your intentions down above, then write them on a piece of paper, or in your journal, so you can visually see them outside yourself. Remember, you transform the energetic pulse of an intention by moving it *out of your brain* and into the tangible world around you. So even the act of scribbling your intention and its corresponding action step on a Post-it note or typing it into your calendar will expand the energetic flow and increase the probability of its fulfillment. We can take that process to an even higher level by creating a ritual around it to prevent your intention from getting lost in the swirl of your day.

CHAPTER ELEVEN

SACRED RITUALS

Though I do not believe that a plant will spring up
where no seed has been, I have great faith in a seed . . .
Convince me that you have a seed there, and I
am prepared to expect wonders.

— Henry David Thoreau

Many of us have specific rituals that we do each morning. Some of us practice yoga, pray, or meditate. Others ask reflective questions or repeat affirmations, and others do heart-opening exercises. These ritualized behaviors are essential to beginning our day on the right path, subtly setting the course that our day will follow.

Starting your day with a meditation ritual provides the perfect environment for your intentions to embed and for your day to unfold with greater grace and greater ease. When we set an intention and go into meditation, it's like planting a seed and then going into the garden to cultivate it with quietude. Now we have a seed pregnant with possibilities, a seed with a built-in manifestation being planted into a vibrationally fertile environment that will help it thrive.

Ritual + Meaning = Transformation

On the following pages, you will crystallize your full embrace of the *Divine Principle of Awareness*, through a series of daily rituals that will create a powerful trajectory for you to move through your day with calm, clarity, decisiveness, and the strength to make new bold, fearless choices. From this moment forward, you will walk this Second Divine Path with grace and ease.

THE DAILY PRACTICES

We can awaken the *Divine Principle of Awareness* in our very core and activate our *Sacred Powers of Attention, Intention,* and *Action* in our life through five transformational daily practices that can be used individually or in combination. Each practice offers you an opportunity to cultivate attention, intention, and action. All five practiced on a daily basis will nourish your powers of transformation:

1. Asking Sacred Questions and Planting Intentions
2. The Garden of Manifestation Meditation
3. Repeating the Sacred Affirmation
4. Performing the Sacred Rite
5. Taking Your Action Step

THE SACRED QUESTIONS

We begin our practice by asking ourselves a few Sacred Questions. These are questions designed to spark a dialogue between you and the Universe. So close your eyes, place your hand over your heart, and silently ask each question for a minute. Sometimes answers will flow. Sometimes there will be no answers. Do not stress out if answers don't come back. It's very common for answers to come back hours or days later. The key is to ask the Sacred Questions over and over until they become part of your inner dialogue. In time they will become part of your outer dialogue, as well, which is how your energy effortlessly transforms.

ASKING SACRED QUESTIONS AND PLANTING INTENTIONS

We begin our day by finding a comfortable place to sit or lie down. So settle in, place your hand on your heart, and begin the practice of asking the Sacred Questions. Simply ask the first question over and over for about a minute, and let answers innocently flow. Don't force it! Then do the same with the second question, then the third. Feel free to spend up to a minute with each question. When you have completed the process, take a long, slow, deep breath in, and release all the questions and any answers that arose. Then invite an intention into your mind. Get clear on it, invite it into your heart, and plant that intention like a seed in the fertile soil of your heart. Then breathe in deeply, and let it go as you exhale. Leave it up to the Universe to work out all the details.

THE THREE SACRED QUESTIONS

To awaken attention, intention, and action in our day, we ask:

What is my deepest desire?

Where can I place my attention today?

What commitment do I make?

Then invite your intention into your awareness. Allow it to crystallize. And when you are clear on it, invite it into your heart. Begin a gentle, slow process of deep breathing as you see it clearly move into your heart; and keep breathing deeply. Envision your endgame, your goal, your target. Notice how manifesting your intention makes you feel . . . in your body, in your mind, in your heart. Slowly witness the progressive steps you will need to take to bring you to that moment—the behaviors, conversations, actions you need to do. What does it look like when it has manifested? How does it feel when it has actually become a reality? Visualize the whole process unfolding from the very first seed until its fulfillment. Own it all. And then plant your intention like a seed deep in your heart. Take a deep breath in to anchor it . . . and let it go. You don't need to think about it anymore. From this moment forward, every time you connect with the stillness and silence inside your heart, you will strengthen the intention and activate its birth in your life.

THE GARDEN OF MANIFESTATION MEDITATION

Now that you've set the table by asking your Sacred Questions, letting answers flow, inviting your intention into your heart, and releasing it out into the Universe, it's time to meditate. Whenever we plant a seed, we first burrow it in fertile soil. Then we water it, and we trust that the seed will grow. When we meditate, we take a Time-In. We allow the outside world to simply be. We release our grip on how we believe everything is supposed to unfold. We till the soil that will hold our seed and make it as fertile as possible. Meditation is our incubation period, where we quiet our body and mind. Once we've planted our intention and released it, we trust the Master Plan of the Universe to work out the details. The Garden of Manifestation Meditation is an ancient technique that sages have used for thousands of years. Early morning practice cultivates the soil of our existence so that our intentions will have a garden to flourish.

There's no equipment necessary. Here's how it works:

1. Find a comfortable place to sit or lie down.

2. Take a long, slow deep breath in, and watch the breath as it moves into you and goes down deep into your belly.

3. Release the breath, and observe it as it moves back out.

4. Continue to slowly and quietly breathe, simply witnessing the process.

5. Once you feel relaxed, begin silently repeating the ancient vibration of manifestation.

    SO HAAM

    As you inhale, silently repeat *SO*. As you exhale, silently repeat *HAAM*. Do it slowly at first and allow a natural pace to take over. There's no perfect speed or cadence—whatever feels right to you.

6. After you've repeated the mantra a few times and found your groove, close your eyes and continue to silently repeat *SO HAAM*.

7. When you notice you have drifted away to thoughts, sounds, and physical sensations (and you will), then gently drift your attention back to *SO HAAM SO HAAM SO HAAM* and continue to silently repeat it.

Let's try it for a minute or two together. I'll wait right here.

How did it feel?

Whether you start each morning with this ritual or meditate for a few minutes here and there throughout the day, every time you practice the Garden of Manifestation Meditation, you are enriching the soil in your own fertile garden so the seeds you have planted deep within have a better chance of sprouting. *SO HAAM*, translated as *I AM*, is one of the oldest Sanskrit mantras in existence. Practicing this meditation on a consistent basis will allow your purest essence to awaken from the inside, transforming your desires, intentions, and dreams into a new magnificent reality.

We spend every minute of our life in activity, from the second we open our eyes to the moment we surrender to the restful dullness of sleep. That span of our daily activity can last from 14 to 18 hours every day, and that can be exhausting. Although sleep rejuvenates our body and our mind, the process of deep sleep is a state of dullness.

Meditation, on the other hand, is a state of restful *awareness.* We are awake and alert, yet in a state of relaxation. This form of nourishment not only boosts your immune system, increases your creativity, heightens your daily performance, and lowers your blood pressure; it also calms your mind so that every seed you've planted feels the release of your grip, inviting the Universe to merge with your intention. In this space of present-moment, restful awareness, there is no anxiety, desperation, or fear. You are truly at your best.

Remember that meditation is a practice, which means that it's an ongoing process. Just as your blood must be pumped through your entire body again and again to keep your cells rich in oxygen, you must keep cultivating the soil of your awareness with stillness and silence. The secret to the practice is to ritual-ize it just as you have ritualized your morning brushing of your teeth and your morning shower routine. So starting every morn-ing with a few minutes of *SO HAAM* will set the perfect trajectory for your day.

If you'd like to learn other meditation techniques, I've included them throughout the book. And I've created a special online guided meditation page exclusively for readers of Sacred Powers so you can close your eyes and fully surrender as I guide you along the Five Divine Paths. Keep reading, and when you're done, visit davidji.com/SacredBonus for free access. Remember: your daily practice can become a powerful friend as you navigate this magnificent journey.

THE SACRED AFFIRMATION

Affirmations are the fertilizer we sprinkle into our soil to ensure our seeds stay nourished. Think about a recent conversation you've had. It wasn't simply an exchange of words between you and another person. Once the conversation was over, you began to judge the interaction—reflecting on the tone, meaning, intent, and resolution of the conversation. Maybe it went really well and you're basking in your victory.

BUT MAYBE IT DIDN'T.

And now, there were all these *after*thoughts and second-guessing, like, "Maybe I sounded foolish." "I hope he understood what I meant." "I should never have said that." "I could have used better words." "I should have waited." "Did I come across as I wanted to?" "What did she mean by . . . ?" We replay conversations over and over in our mind, conjuring hundreds of thoughts about something that the other person most likely has forgotten. We call this torturous rehashing of the past *ruminating*.

Usually, the playback of our daily interactions generate some non-nourishing thoughts—sparking destructive emotions such as fear, anger, jealousy, shame, anxiety, regret, guilt, or inferiority. They take up space. They get in the way of our transformation. They make us play small or not at all. They hinder us on our path of growth, expansion, love, and fulfillment.

But remember: thoughts are choices we make in our mind. And we can choose how we want our mind to work. Do we want to see each moment as a grievance or a miracle? And even if we don't necessarily desire a miracle in that moment, we always have a choice between wallowing in non-nourishing self-talk or bathing in life-affirming thoughts.

THE POWER OF AFFIRMATIONS

Affirmations are powerful because they can override our conditioned doubts, uncertainties, and fears to shake us out of a mind-set of less-than thinking. They effortlessly interrupt the patterns and behaviors that haven't really served us through most of our life. They are transformational because they convert energy! They diminish negative self-talk and reinforce life-affirming intentions. They become our inner voice, which ultimately evolves into our persona. And so what once started as a negative internal conversation, gets overridden by a positive, elevating dialogue between you and your highest self. With continued attention, our silent self-expression grows and blossoms and blooms. As an ancient sage once said, "All that we are arises with our thoughts; with our thoughts, we create the world." Silently repeating your *Sacred Affirmation* throughout the day gives you the spontaneous ability to re-create your world!

To keep the *Divine Principle of Awareness* thriving in our life, strengthening our intentions, and moving into the best version of our self, we repeat the *Sacred Affirmation*:

I am the master of this moment; what I seek, I already am!

THE SACRED RITE

We've asked the *Sacred Questions*, we've planted an intention for the day, and we've drifted into stillness and silence to incubate our seed. We've invoked our daily affirmation to keep the *Divine Principle of Awareness* fresh and available in every moment. And you can take it even deeper by practicing a sacred physical rite—essentially a *power move*—that will set the tone for the day and keep you on track whenever you get overwhelmed, disappointed, anxious, or drift away from the single-point of your intention.

It's a combination of a thought, word, and physical action. You can invoke your power move to start your day, whenever you feel self-doubt creep into your mind, or at structured intervals throughout the day like 10 A.M., noon, 2 P.M., 4 P.M., and right before you go to bed. The blend of thought, word, and physical movement will connect all those aspects of your brain, merging your body and mind with the flow of the Universe. It's one more way to stoke the energetic flow of your dreams and desires.

Think to yourself the affirmation of the day, in this case:

I am the master of this moment; what I seek, I already am!

Then imagine you are an archer, holding a bow in your left hand. Raise your left arm, parallel to the ground, and move your right hand to meet your left wrist and pull back on an invisible string as if you were going to fire an arrow. Hold that imaginary arrow tight, pulling your string all the back to the right side of your chin. Close your left eye, and aim your arrow at the target of your dream out into the direction of the unknown, either far into the distance or up to the heavens. And as you release your arrow, whisper, say, or shout the word *clarity*.

You can practice this sacred rite for the *Divine Principle of Awareness* at any time throughout the day, whether you are sitting, standing, about to enter a meeting—even while you are lying in bed.

TAKING YOUR ACTION STEP

We have practiced the Sacred Rituals for walking the *Divine Path of Awareness*. But, without taking action, none of our good intentions will manifest. We need to lean in the direction of our dream, and lean hard. We do this by simply taking a step today, tomorrow, and the next day. Once we have taken action for three consecutive days, the fourth day is easy, and then the fifth. And before you know it, we have introduced a brand-new behavior into our week. And as you see the incremental results, you will realize that baby step by baby step, your life is slowly transforming. Action is how we turn concept into reality to move the physical Universe in the direction of our dream. So, with everything you've learned as you've walked the *Divine Path of Awareness*, write down the Action Step you will take today, tomorrow, and the day after. Remember: baby steps! Follow this blueprint for the next three days, and you'll feel your transformation starting to take hold.

Begin this process by first saying out loud, "Here I am in this precious, sacred present moment. What will I do to honor it?" And then fill in the answers:

Action Step for Today

Today I Will

_____

Action Step for Tomorrow

Tomorrow I Will

_____

Action Step for the Day After Tomorrow

In Two Days I Will

_____

Doesn't that feel amazing? Action is the acceleration of your transformation!

THE DIVINE PRINCIPLE OF REBIRTH

The Divine Principle of REbirth
and
the Sacred Powers of
Acceptance, Release, and
New Beginnings

CHAPTER TWELVE

WALKING THE THIRD DIVINE PATH

Returning to Stardust

When I let go of who I am, I become who I might be.

— Lao-tzu

With Every Breath I Am Reborn

We all would like to turn back the clock to a moment in time or simply push the reset button to see if we might have better luck the second time around. In golf, it's called a mulligan when your first shot goes into the woods, and you give yourself a second chance by teeing the ball up one more time. In dermatology, it's called rejuvenation, when the damage of a lifetime of aging is repaired and damaged tissues are replaced.

But we are multidimensional Beings. And for most of us, the new beginnings we seek are far beyond hitting a golf ball or renewing our skin cells. We seek the true REbirthing of many aspects of our emotional, physical, psychological, and spiritual selves. We long for the creation of new memories, new desires, new choices, and new dreams. You've learned a lot over the course of your life. And if you could apply all that wisdom to your current circumstances and have a fresh start in just one area, your life would truly transform in magnificent ways.

REbirth is a *spiritual homecoming*—our returning to the memory of our wholeness before we carved out all the ruts, climbed the mountains, crawled up from the abysses, trudged across the valleys, slid down the hills, and fell down rabbit holes. All these experiences have provided strength and wisdom, but we don't need to hold on to the staleness of their trajectory. *Even in the smallest of issues and the tiniest of concerns, you are worthy of a second chance.* You are entitled to a new beginning!

THE MEMORY OF YOUR WHOLENESS

For thousands of years, various wisdom traditions have sought that one special thing that would bring about a return to the moment of our birth. In ancient China, it was the quest for a mystical pearl with special powers; in the Gospel of John, it was the Pool of Bethesda, where Jesus restored invalids to their healed, whole state; in medieval times, it was consulting with the wizard and searching for the Holy Grail. Then there were the legendary alchemists of Europe, who pursued the mystical Philosopher's Stone, supposedly capable of turning mercury into gold, rejuvenating the body, and gifting the holder with immortality.

Thousands of years before all these fabled quests for eternal life, the ancient healers and masters of the Soul were already walking the *Divine Path of REbirth* and uncovering its timeless secrets. In their ancient wisdom, they understood this journey as a sacred process of initiation, in which our true REbirth unfolds from within. They cultivated the knowledge of how to connect to source, awaken the memory of our wholeness, and flow our most divine selves back out into the world.

They trained a select few, in a powerful practice of physical, emotional, and spiritual deconstruction (how to release everything that no longer served them) and total reconstruction (building from scratch every component of their existence piece by piece). They taught that we have the innate ability to accept all that has happened, fully release the constricting aspects of it, and take fresh, bold steps into a new trajectory of life.

REbirth is possible if we give ourselves permission to gently, lovingly, openly, and tenderly peel away the layers of our bodies, our minds, and our Souls to reveal that sweet, pure perfection that is at the center of our being.

Your journey of REbirth starts with fully embracing the *Divine Principle of REbirth* as a Universal law and then connecting to the true source of it within yourself. Once you're in that place, you can radiate that energy back out into the world to weave the fabric of a healed, whole, beautiful brand-new existence.

How Awake Is Your *Power* of REbirth?

Your ability to be REborn rests at the very core of your existence—the initial seed of stardust that first breathed life into you. But right now, it's resting dormant in the quietest recesses of your soul, cloaked in darkness by a lifetime of conditioning, waiting to be awakened. So, before we dive in deeper, let's find out how asleep it truly is, by taking the pulse of your REbirth-ability.

This simple exercise will bring you instant clarity as you drill down into the key areas of your life. Use the following questions to fill in the boxes on the next several pages to assess your power of REbirth in each of the five realms: Physical, Emotional, Material, Relationship, and Spiritual.

First: On a scale of 1 to 10, rate how important or pressing each aspect of your life is to you right now. A way to spark the process is to ask yourself,

Right now, how much attention am I placing on this area of my life?

1 = no attention; 10 = constant attention.
Enter these numbers into the boxes in the first column.

Next: On a scale of 1 to 10, rate how satisfied you are with this aspect of your life. Ask yourself,

How satisfied am I with this aspect of my life?

1 = totally unsatisfied; 10 = totally satisfied.
Enter these numbers into the boxes in the second column.

And last: on a scale of 1 to 10, rate your desire for REbirth by asking,

How deeply do I desire a new trajectory in this aspect of my life?

1 = no desire; 10 = extreme desire.
Enter these numbers into the boxes in the third column.

Physical Realm (every aspect of your physical body)			
	My Current Attention	Satisfaction Level	Desire for REbirth
General health	☐	☐	☐
Stomach/digestion	☐	☐	☐
Rest	☐	☐	☐
Teeth	☐	☐	☐
Energy	☐	☐	☐
Mental stimulation	☐	☐	☐
Self-image	☐	☐	☐
Aging	☐	☐	☐
Pain	☐	☐	☐
Sleep	☐	☐	☐
Sex	☐	☐	☐
Exercise	☐	☐	☐
Diet	☐	☐	☐
Non-nourishing habits	☐	☐	☐
Other physical issues: _____	☐	☐	☐

Emotional Realm (how you respond when your needs are not met)			
	My Current Attention	Satisfaction Level	Desire for REbirth
Empathy	☐	☐	☐
Anger	☐	☐	☐
Sadness	☐	☐	☐
Jealousy	☐	☐	☐
Regret	☐	☐	☐
Self-worth	☐	☐	☐
Confidence	☐	☐	☐
Patience	☐	☐	☐
Happiness	☐	☐	☐
Joy	☐	☐	☐
Celebration	☐	☐	☐
Judgment	☐	☐	☐
Gratitude	☐	☐	☐
Defensiveness	☐	☐	☐
Other emotional issues: _____	☐	☐	☐

Material Realm (positions and possessions)			
	My Current Attention	Satisfaction Level	Desire for REbirth
Career or job	☐	☐	☐
Income	☐	☐	☐
Savings	☐	☐	☐
Financial security	☐	☐	☐
Insurance	☐	☐	☐
Sense of safety	☐	☐	☐
Residence	☐	☐	☐
Possessions	☐	☐	☐
Car	☐	☐	☐
Debt	☐	☐	☐
Furniture	☐	☐	☐
Clothes	☐	☐	☐
Worry over stuff	☐	☐	☐
Abundance mind-set	☐	☐	☐
Other material issues: _____	☐	☐	☐

Relationship Realm (the birthing, repairing, shifting, and fresh start of connections you have with those in your life)

	My Current Attention	Satisfaction Level	Desire for REbirth
Self-love	☐	☐	☐
Self-trust	☐	☐	☐
Front row	☐	☐	☐
Feeling supported	☐	☐	☐
Forgiveness	☐	☐	☐
Core relationship	☐	☐	☐
Ex	☐	☐	☐
Close friends	☐	☐	☐
Pets	☐	☐	☐
Family	☐	☐	☐
Co-workers	☐	☐	☐
Community	☐	☐	☐
Non-nourishing relationships	☐	☐	☐
Stuck relationships	☐	☐	☐
Other relationship issues: _____	☐	☐	☐

Spiritual Realm (how the Universe flows through you, your basic nature, your connection to Spirit)		
	My Current Attention	Satisfaction Level	Desire for REbirth
Creativity	☐	☐	☐
Self-actualization	☐	☐	☐
Time in nature	☐	☐	☐
Compassion	☐	☐	☐
Peak experiences	☐	☐	☐
Detachment	☐	☐	☐
Faith	☐	☐	☐
Acceptance	☐	☐	☐
Charity	☐	☐	☐
Daily meditation practice	☐	☐	☐
Acts of kindness	☐	☐	☐
Trusting the Universe	☐	☐	☐
Understanding my purpose	☐	☐	☐
Relationship with higher power	☐	☐	☐
Other spiritual issues: _____	☐	☐	☐

WHERE'S MY ATTENTION?

After you have filled in every box, scan through all five realms of your life and see where your attention has mostly been. All these issues are important in our lives; however, some of them absolutely have greater relevance in a given moment. For example, in the Physical Realm—if you've just gone to the dentist and your teeth are in great shape, then you can comfortably drift your attention away from this area and give the "Teeth" category a 1 under *My Current Attention*, 10 under *Satisfaction Level*, and 1 under *Desire for REbirth*. Nice job!

On the other hand, in the Relationship Realm—if you've just had an argument with a close friend, loved one, or work colleague, then this situation would rate a 9 or 10 under *My Current Attention*, a 1 or 2 under *Satisfaction Level*, and probably a 9 or 10 in terms of *Desire for REbirth*. This would be an area that is causing you acute emotional pain, and it would benefit by being addressed right now.

Your high-attention areas are where the majority of your 70,000 thoughts a day have been concentrated. If there are areas of your life that you feel are important to you but your attention has been elsewhere, it's because other high-attention areas are stealing your energy. In every moment, we get to choose where we want to place our energy. If you feel that you haven't been giving your best to certain areas, it's not because you don't care. It's because you are allowing other, less important issues to hijack your attention.

SUFFERING, SURVIVING, OR THRIVING?

Over the past few decades, the concepts of suffering, surviving, and thriving in the workplace have been explored in hundreds of business books. Yet we rarely apply that same lens to our own personal life. Maybe it's because we have been taught that suffering is part of life. But, as you scan your answers in the *Satisfaction Level* column, you may suddenly realize that you have low levels of satisfaction in areas that are important to you—areas where you truly desire a REbirth. We can't thrive all the time in every area of our life, but we can absolutely find balance. And we can make appropriate shifts in our choice making that will guarantee that we are at least surviving in every area of our life. Suffering is optional.

YOUR DESIRE FOR REBIRTH

Now scan the *Desire for REbirth* column from top to bottom. If the number is under 5, it most likely means you are content with your current state of affairs regarding that issue. If the numbers are higher, these are areas of your life in which you are yearning for a fresh start and where you need to begin the process of REbirth. If your levels of satisfaction are low and your desire for REbirth is high, then this is the sweet spot of your transformation. In these cases, a deeper reflection needs to be explored. How much attention are you placing on this aspect of your life? If it's already a lot, then you are directing your attention to the wrong aspect of the problem and you simply need to get a little more creative with your solution. If, on the other hand, your attention is also low, now you have some spiritual tools to help you. Simply awakening your *Sacred Power of Attention* could solve the whole issue. You may also want to ask yourself a few deeply reflective questions, such as: "Why is my attention not on this aspect of my life?" "Do I wish it was there, but I just can't seem to get to it?" "Or is my desire for REbirth in this area just a *momentary* pain point from being too sensitive or overreactive?"

Another possible outcome of the exercise is that you've rated something very high on your *Current Attention* yet low on your *Desire for REbirth*. This could mean you are spending a lot of thought and energy on something simply to keep the status quo. For example, let's say that you love your job, even though it consumes the majority of your attention, but you don't wish it to evolve or grow (otherwise, you would have rated it higher under *Desire for REbirth*).

These are simply areas where you can work smarter rather than harder and possibly delegate some of your chores or activities to someone else or figure out ways to be more efficient. This is where you ask yourself, "How can I keep things running as they are without so much of my attention?" Remember, we only have a finite amount of attention that we can place on any one aspect of our life. And if we want to shift something in our life, we need to shine the flashlight of attention on it.

REbirth doesn't mean that you have to blow something up completely, or even start from scratch. You simply need to stop whatever you were doing—which was not aligned with the Universe—and start leaning in a new direction where you are divinely supported.

Now that you've taken your REbirth pulse, clarity is unfolding. So let's keep walking this *Third Divine Path of REbirth* and move deeper into the foundation of what actually brought you to this defining moment.

CHAPTER THIRTEEN

THE TAMING OF YOUR SOUL

You were once wild here. Don't let them tame you.

— Isadora Duncan

HOW YOU GOT TO THIS AUSPICIOUS MOMENT

You were born whole, perfect, pure, and enlightened—one tiny foot resting in the womb of your existence and the other reaching into this physical world. For nine months, you were nurtured— fed, warmed, soothed, hydrated, nourished, and protected from all outside issues. All of your needs were met as you rested in the cradle of the Divine. And as you emerged from Source and took your first breath of life through air, your powerful first moment of personal individuation unfolded. But it's been a few years since that sacred moment.

In your first moments of birth, you were defenseless, vulnerable, and truly bursting with infinite possibilities. Then, suddenly, the harsh reality that all of your needs would not be automatically met set in. Instead of merging with your mother for sleep, food, warmth, and comfort, you needed to announce every unmet need and hope that someone would assist you in meeting it.

And so, need by need, urge by urge, desire by desire, thought by thought, and thread by thread, you wove a tapestry of how you would interact with the world. Squirming, crying, grunting, and giggling soon gave way to more articulate expressions as you recognized who and what would bring you comfort in a given moment. You tried your hardest to please those around you so they would feed you, bathe you, clean your diaper, hold you, and love you.

You developed patterns of conditioned behavior, and soon your physiological and biological prerequisites evolved into more complex emotional requests. Your needs of the heart began to awaken in a more intricate way. You began making interpretations and guesses about how situations should unfold and what others thought, believed, and did. And then, at a certain point, you naturally assumed that all of us thought the same things, felt the same way, and had the same motives behind our actions.

As we grew older, our core needs of attention, affection, appreciation, and acceptance became more overt, and we began weaving them into that tapestry of interrelatedness with our parents, siblings, relatives, friends, schoolmates, and work colleagues. Our vocabulary may have evolved over time, but these needs of the heart stayed the same—and our ingrained, underdeveloped emotional responses stayed locked in the past.

We continued to build on everything that had come before. All of our interpretations, guesses, successes, confusions, disappointments, and miscalculations were simply extensions of those very first fibers we threaded into the world.

REFINING OUR PERSONA

My dear Nagual friend don Miguel Ruiz, Sr., the brilliant author of *The Four Agreements*, refers to this early self-creation process as a form of *self-domestication*. And for the most part, our constant reinforcement of our earliest responses is a self-taming progression, a tailoring of how we will show up in the world for the rest of our lives. Essentially, we craft an identity, like a character in a book or a role we will play, that moves through all the phases of our life—

all the while expanding, constricting, and refining that persona. We do what we need to do in order to receive the attention, affection, appreciation, and acceptance we so desperately crave.

Many of us play it safe; others take risks. But it's all experimental because these choices are mostly happening *in real time.* We accept the basic rules from our parents, teachers, caregivers, and authority figures and we cultivate what we believe will be our "formula." We evolve into who we think we need to be and how we will need to act, speak, and behave in order to be successful in all the different areas of our life.

In some cases, we thrive and soar. And, in others, it's a dumbing down of our best expression. As we learn a little bit more about how life "works," we justify certain choices by telling ourselves little white lies like "It will get better after this," "I only need to pretend in this moment," "If I say this or do this, I'll receive more attention, affection, appreciation, or acceptance." In our weakest moments, we start to forget that we're this pure, whole, perfect being who came into this world filled with infinite possibilities. Out of fear or desperation, we make decisions that box us into corners we never expected to find ourselves in. Over time, it becomes the new normal; suddenly, we are making life choices based on someone else's intentions and desires. In those uncertain moments, so far from our original plan, we defer our dreams and resign ourselves to accepting smaller expressions of our magnificence until our once-bright light begins to dim.

Granted, it can be pretty scary when we arrive at the doorstep of the unknown. In moments where we find ourselves wavering or questioning our choices, we often lack the patience or confidence to allow the situation to unfold organically. We stop trusting that the Universe will provide all the answers and lovingly deliver us to exactly where we need to be. Instead, we self-interrogate whether it is indeed the right place, or if it's the right time, or what we could have done differently to arrive at a different outcome—one with less uncertainty, pain, distress, or anxiety.

BUILDING WALLS

As the years go on, we forget that divine moment of our birth and get further and further away from our innate knowledge of our wholeness, perfection, and purity. With each mistake or regretful action, we stop *accepting* that we are divine creations. We begin to build walls in our heart, our conversations, our sense of self, our attitudes, and even in our physical body. Our fear of being judged makes us seek to fit in, and our natural state of self-acceptance and self-celebration starts to fade. We become masters of hiding our vulnerability behind masks of stoicism and projections of false confidence. And in the process we lose the precious gift of our innocence and become skeptical of the infinite kindness of the Universe.

Drinking all this in at once can seem pretty bleak. But our self-domestication is all part of the human condition. And this is how the divinity in our Soul is tamed. We all respond differently to this process, but everyone goes through these moments, and everyone makes compromises—big and small. This is the story of everyone.

And right now, whatever path you have taken to get here, you hold at your fingertips the power to turn it all around—the power of REbirth, renewal, and reinvention.

THE POWER OF REBIRTH

It's a powerful aha moment when we suddenly realize that we are all thinking and living from a giant collective brain—yet looking at life through our own unique lens and making very personal and individual choices based on our own perception of reality.

In that sacred, precious moment when we fully understand that we are the only ones paying real close attention to every one of our thoughts, dreams, desires, words, and actions, our worldview, and our world transform forever. *We realize that there is no council of elders taking notes on our every thought, judging our every move, chronicling it down for all eternity to inspect. In that defining breakthrough moment of clarity, we give ourselves permission to venture out again from the womb of life, be birthed again, and reinvent ourselves and our universe.*

And that is why the concept and the practice of REbirth has resonated with so many for thousands of years. There is no more profound initiation into a new beginning than the act of birth. And the sacred birthing ceremonies of these ancient civilizations have been carried forward into our modern era with rituals that include bathing, washing, shaving the head, anointment with oil, adornment of the body with ash or paint, and even receiving a new name.

OUT OF THE FIRE

Adversity can also be the seed of REbirth. Pain can be a powerful motivator. Sometimes in the wake of a tragedy, trauma, or un-expected disappointment, we can dig deep—deeper than we ever imagined—and step beyond our preconceived limitations. Our ca-pacity to rebound after we've been dealt a blow is called resilience. And those who embrace their sacred powers and practice healing modalities seem to recover more quickly. Studies show that those practicing these life tools reach out more readily for support, en-couragement, and treatment, breaking the cycle of chronic stress.

As the German philosopher Friedrich Nietzsche wrote in his 1889 book *Twilight of the Idols*, "That which does not kill us, makes us stronger." More than 100 years later, pop singer Kelly Clark-son echoed Nietzsche's sentiment in her hit about thriving after heartbreak—"Stronger (What Doesn't Kill You)." In fact, modern psychological research has now developed a term for those who defy post-traumatic stress disorder (PTSD), get stronger, and step into their power after a loss or traumatic incident. The scientific community now refers to it as post-traumatic growth (PTG).

REBIRTH = RESILIENCY

This powerful shift in biological stress response has been linked to increased wound healing, improved relationships with those who lend support, a crystallized sense of appreciation for life, and deeper gratitude for those in it. In many cases, those experiencing the trauma raise their pain threshold, allowing them to be stron-ger and even more resilient in the face of additional traumas.

I experienced this in my youth after my mother died unexpectedly. In the depth of my pain and confusion, I rationalized, "Nothing this bad could ever happen to me again, no matter what!" That gave me a spark of courage to risk looking foolish, try new things when the pressure was on, and take bold or unpopular steps. I was infused with the strength of PTG one more time in the aftermath of 9/11, after those I had worked with in Tower Two of the World Trade Center lost their lives.

YOU ARE BEING CALLED

As you continue to cultivate the *Divine Principle of REbirth*, you will see that defining moments like these are heavenly invitations from the Universe to take ownership of your life, step into your power, and leap into your REbirth. Eleanor Roosevelt reinforced this sentiment when she said, "You gain strength, courage and confidence by every experience in which you really stop to look fear in the face. You are able to say to yourself, 'I have lived through this horror. I can take the next thing that comes along.' You must do the thing you think you cannot do."

Way down deep in your heart, do you feel yourself being called? Are you willing to step into your best version? I think you are.

So let's give it a go. What's the worst that could happen? What's the best that could happen? Your REbirth begins by first activating the *Sacred Power of Acceptance*, essentially claiming and owning every aspect of your life. If we don't claim the past—*and claim it all*—we can't claim the REbirth. So, to truly accept, you need to first *give your self permission to take ownership* of every moment of your life, from the moment you first breathed air right up to this very breath. It's intense, I know. But take the leap with me right now. The best is yet to come. I promise. So if you're ready, we'll start walking the *Divine Path of REbirth* by exploring an ancient deconstruction process known as the Divine Formula.

CHAPTER FOURTEEN

THE DIVINE FORMULA

The people who don't ask questions
remain clueless throughout their lives.

— Neil deGrasse Tyson

WHAT'S YOUR WINNING FORMULA?

As a child, sometime between your 5th birthday and your 15th birthday, you made the first of many powerful, defining life decisions.

You dreamed of becoming something, so you attempted it for the very first time, but you were met with resistance. Maybe it just didn't work out as you planned or there was something or someone in your way. Perhaps it was a friend, sibling, or schoolmate who you thought was smarter, better looking, more popular, or got all the breaks. Perhaps it was an authority figure who told you that you weren't smart enough or a relative that said you couldn't succeed. You witnessed someone in your life receiving the attention, affection, appreciation, or acceptance you craved. And they seemed to receive it effortlessly. Maybe it seemed to you that others were offered all the opportunities you couldn't get. Or perhaps you had ingrained a limiting belief so deeply into your persona that it officially outlined all the boundaries of what you believed was possible. Bottom line: to overcome and transcend the challenges of life, *you made a choice to define yourself a certain way.*

POLISHING YOUR CONTACT LENSES

In essence, you developed your own personal *Winning Formula*, a way to see and interpret the world as if you were wearing a one-of-a-kind set of contact lenses that had been ground and polished to fit only your eyes. And with each subtle, unconscious decision you made—and the millions of subsequent decisions you chose reinforcing it—you honed and perfected the lenses as you refined your Winning Formula. You sanded them, buffed them, and engrained them with your limiting beliefs, your fears, and your conditioned responses. Ultimately, you became unable to see anything other than what your customized contact lenses projected. And from that moment forward, your Winning Formula took over. Essentially, you said, "This is how I will deal with life; this is how I will show up; this is who I will be." And so you tamed yourself to navigate the roadblocks and speed bumps of life.

#WINNING

As a child, because I felt I did not have a voice at home or receive the attention I craved, I cultivated a Winning Formula based on being funny. I realized early on that people respond to humor, and that if I injected comedy into a given moment, I would receive the attention I felt I wouldn't otherwise receive. My Winning Formula began as the occasional joker, then the class clown, and evolved into being the person who always had a quip ready. As I grew up, I developed an affable nature and reinforced it with my winning formula, which fueled my leadership skills in school. I was voted class president and then head of the student council. My winning formula helped me receive attention from my peers, fellow students, and teachers—the attention I so desperately craved, but did not receive at home. Because I was considered funny, I was invited into social circles, academic clubs, and bonded with my professors, which inspired me to study harder. That led to great scores on my tests and solid grades, which in turn helped me get into some fine universities with academic cred after high school. But, even when I was awarded the National Merit Scholarship for Academic Excellence, at my acceptance ceremony, the dean asked, "Do you have a joke to tell us?" All this reinforced my commitment to my winning formula.

STILL WINNING

And the trend continued. After I left school, in the development and reinforcement of my "Winning" Formula, I received the attention, affection, appreciation, and acceptance from my clients, partners, work colleagues, and bosses. In time, even the media began paying attention to me, and soon I was playing on a global stage.

Success unfolded for me in the world of business, as I leveraged my winning formula of humor, adding a lightheartedness to each moment that balanced the more serious, heaviness of my stereotypical type A, Taurus, New York style. It guaranteed that I could always get a word into any conversation, that people would listen to me, and most likely enjoy my company. But I never felt as if they were really *listening;* they were hearing only the joke. My humorous persona came to define me, and my contact lenses were so tightly stuck to my eyes, I had no other way to validate my existence than through other people's laughter. It was the only way I could guarantee that I'd received the attention, affection, appreciation, and acceptance of the world around me. That's why I had originally planted that initial seed of my winning formula so many years before. I was just so desperately afraid to risk being liked or loved for just being me.

YOUR GREATEST STRENGTH
IS ALSO YOUR GREATEST WEAKNESS!

I had become a master at my winning formula, and it colored everything I thought, said, and did. It was the contact lens I saw the world through—so close, that I didn't even realize it was there. I had conditioned myself—or to use don Miguel's phrase, I had "domesticated" myself. Essentially, I had tamed myself to *always respond with humor ultimately crafting my persona.* But what did it cost me? It cost me my heart, my authenticity, my vulnerability. It cost me intimacy. It cost me the fact that my true voice had never been heard—because I had never trusted that it would be enough. My contact lenses had been so finely polished that my ego, self-worth, and self-esteem depended on whether or not someone laughed while in my presence. And here's the rub: I used that very fact to offset my behavior when I was harsh, reactive, insensitive, or impatient. I rationalized in my mind that since I made so many people laugh, smile, or feel good over the course of the day, that it more than offset my more unattractive behaviors. But, deep down, I felt brokenhearted, isolated, and afraid to express my most authentic self.

TRUTH ALWAYS RESTS AT THE SOURCE

There was obviously deeper pain that had not worked its way out of me. Rather than addressing it, I had sugarcoated my childhood issues of loneliness, emptiness, worthiness, self-love, and relevance. Instead of being the soft, tender, kinder person I truly wanted to be in my heart of hearts, I had built a fortress to protect me from my deepest, most painful emotions. I had created a powerful excuse to *not* grow, *not* evolve, and *not* transform. My Winning Formula had devolved into my *Losing* Formula!

The personal paradigm I created as a child so that I could succeed in life was costing me as I grew up. What had delivered me to a pinnacle of "success" right up until my 35th birthday, was now holding me back from being the best version of myself. When I looked in the mirror, I did not see myself as smart, thoughtful, insightful, intelligent, authentic, compassionate, helpful, loving, or supportive—the fundamental traits that I held dear as my Sacred Values. Instead I defined myself as simply *funny*. Yes. For 30 years, my winning formula had brought me the trappings of what many consider success—a steady paycheck, a loving family, a posse of friends. To look at my life, I should have had everything. But I was miserable. Inside, I was feeling shallow, small, and alone.

Over time I realized that I had built a barrier to receiving love in my heart; I had dumbed down my ability to authentically flow it back out into the world; and I was missing the true depth of connection.

THE SPARK OF ACCEPTANCE—TAKING OWNERSHIP OF YOUR LIFE

And so it was necessary to recraft my vision of the world as I saw my life unfolding over the next one, three, five years—essentially emotionally deconstructing and then reconstructing myself. In his self- reflective book, *An Invented Life*, the American scholar and teacher Warren Bennis explains, "I believe in self invention. I have to believe in it . . . To be authentic is to literally be your own author . . . to discover your native energies and desires, and find your way of acting on them." As I read those words, I knew in my heart it was time to REbirth and change my winning formula. And that phrase—*"To be authentic is to literally be your own author"*—had just given me the permission I craved! I needed to come back to my core . . . my heart . . . my truth . . . and step into what Bennis referred to as my "native energies and desires," essentially my most vulnerable self.

WHEN I LET GO OF WHO I AM

In that moment, I began the process of taking responsibility for all of my life choices from the moment I first stepped from the womb. That was the key. I forgave the little boy who so long ago had made that desperate choice to build a protective wall of humor around his heart. Instead I learned to appreciate him, grateful that he had brought me to my current state. And now here I stood on the platform of my own making, recognizing that what got me here was not going to take me to the next level. But by finally celebrating the innocent little boy inside me who had tried to keep me safe by taking responsibility for every choice I had made along the way—*by releasing the joker who had shielded me from the native energy in my heart*—I was able to take back my power and fully REbirth.

I've never publicly spoken or written so candidly about my past, or the steps I took to REbirth myself. But I feel that you'll better grasp this process once you know the rawness of the pain that I've moved through. Hopefully, my vulnerability will help you go deeper into your own journey of REbirth.

POLISHING THE MIRROR

Once I realized I had been looking at so much of my life through this distorted contact lens, I took it out, wiped it clean, and dedicated myself to seeing with "new eyes." To break the cycle of my conditioning, I needed a powerful pattern interrupt, so I began meditating twice a day—first thing in the morning and at the end of my day. I developed a gentle morning ritual to open my heart, flow gratitude, and awaken my sacred powers. I made forgiveness an important part of my interactions, embracing the ancient practice of self-kindness, known in the Buddhist traditions as maitrī (pronounced may-tree). I immersed into daily emotional healing practices. I surrendered fully to my native energies to flow my most authentic self. And I began to truly live the *Five Divine Principles*.

And rather than trying to get people to laugh, I found my validation in sharing timeless wisdom. I cultivated a gentle teaching process that was powerful, yet lighthearted, so that my students throughout the world could integrate the depth of this profound knowledge into their own lives with a smile. As my style crystallized, I realized that I was so much more deeply fulfilled by nods of understanding than by giggles. It didn't happen overnight. I had many missteps and false starts along the way. But when I got to the point where I had truly awakened my Sacred Powers, authenticity flowed, and the life I had always dreamed about effortlessly revealed itself.

NO EQUIPMENT NECESSARY . . . ONLY TRUST

Like any birth, the process of REbirth can include some prickly discomfort as you hold the mirror up. It requires total self-honesty. But the end result is a magnificent liberation. So, please trust the process I'm about to lead you through.

The Divine Principle of REbirth has existed for eternity. And there are three sacred powers that have upheld this timeless truth of renewal since man and womankind first walked the earth.

Awakening them connects you more closely to the Universe, frees you from emotional constriction, and helps you to step into your power:

The Sacred Power of Acceptance

The Sacred Power of Release

The Sacred Power of New Beginnings

So let's open the door to the *Divine Principle of REbirth*, and walk this magnificent path together by first awakening the Sacred Power of Acceptance in our lives.

CHAPTER FIFTEEN

THE SACRED POWER
OF ACCEPTANCE

*The art of acceptance is the art of making someone
who has just done you a small favor wish that he
might have done you a greater one.*

— Russell Lynes

THE THREE LEVELS OF ACCEPTANCE

Acceptance is a beautiful teaching with many different levels. It is
the root and the foundation of many wisdom traditions including
Buddhist compassion teachings, the ancient Hindu *Law of Least
Effort*, and Christ Consciousness. But regardless of your orientation to these belief systems, you can find powerful, personal evolution by awakening the *Sacred Power of Acceptance* in your life.
There are three core levels of acceptance, and we instantly shift
every aspect of our being by:

LEVEL 1. Accepting that this moment is perfect, pure,
whole, and every moment that has led to this moment
was exactly the way it was meant to be. This moment is
the magnificent culmination of all of your life choices;
every experience that has woven itself in, around, and

through you; and every one of the 31 million seconds that have ticked by in just this year alone! It couldn't be any other way.

LEVEL 2. Accepting that *you* are a divine being who is sealed in this human body for the span of a lifetime and that you have made choices and decisions throughout your life from your highest level of consciousness at the time. Even though there are choices you may regret or torture yourself about, they are carved in stone and you must accept them, forgive yourself, and make better choices in the future.

LEVEL 3. Accepting others for who they are and not as we wish they would be. Allowing people's differences, quirks, unique vibrations to just be and not necessarily fit into our box of how the world is supposed to be. Allowing others to be as they are.

When you awaken the *Sacred Power of Acceptance*, you finally recognize that wherever you are, every moment of the past is carved in stone and for you to evolve your life, improve your situation, or find deeper fulfillment you must own the present moment.

Level 2 is where so many of us get stuck. By nature, we are our own toughest critic; we know all the moments where we felt less-than, or were sloppy, lazy, or casual with our words or decisions. We know those times when we were unsure of which road to take and we guessed "wrong." We know where we could have been better, or stronger, or wiser, or more patient, or more truthful, or more engaged. But in that moment, we didn't know it. We didn't have access to a crystal ball showing us the consequences; or maybe we didn't take the time to really explore the depth of our actions or choices.

So right now we have two very clear ways to live life. We can either:

1. Beat ourselves up for not being clairvoyant and diminish the happiness in our lives by pointing a continuous finger of blame at ourselves; or

2. Accept the past as a lesson—a profound preparation for all that is to come—so that we can make better choices and find deeper fulfillment in life.

THE BLAME GAME

So often, we hold ourselves accountable for all the pitfalls and unhappiness in our lives and we point to some decision we made that was the root of it all. But this is unnecessary and harsh. And building up the blame case has no value except in a courtroom. In the real world, where a judge or jury of our momentary choices doesn't exist, attributing blame only gets in the way of making the best decision in this moment. Especially self-blame because that is also self-defeating. It takes the wind out of our sails, and that doesn't help us in any way.

In business, in history, in politics, and in sports, the stakes are so high that the ability to step beyond the moment of blame and accept our individual missteps, mistakes, and misspeaks separates the winners from the losers. The ability to accept the fact that we did our best from our own level of consciousness at the time separates those willing to step out of the past (which is the stale, the old, the stuck) and into the present (which is rich, fresh, and filled with infinite opportunities). Those mired in self-pity or finger-pointing are trapped in the past and destined to stay there because they will not accept what is already carved in stone. They remain paralyzed in self-finger-pointing mode and that becomes their excuse for why they are unfulfilled. While those who have owned and accepted their decisions are able to move forward and make new, proud, exciting, restorative choices. We can keep complaining about the rain, or accept that it's raining and find an umbrella.

We get to choose. We are choice-making beings. No one can ever take that away from us—not even ourselves. We just need a little reminder now and then.

When you resist, you block the natural flow of the Universe. It's like crossing your arms just as someone is about to hug you. Picture that in your mind's eye right now. On the other hand, acceptance is not simply uncrossing your arms; rather, it's the proactive invitation for something new to come into you. Acceptance creates the starting point of the *Divine Principle of REbirth*. Acceptance is the moment that you give yourself permission to *truly own* every aspect of your existence, merging with every single moment that has led up to this moment. The great author, teacher, publisher, and champion of emotional healing Louise Hay, who popularized the concept of affirmations, has been quoted many times as saying, "All is well."

Sacred Questions

We can begin the journey of emotional freedom, REbirth, and self-evolution by taking some quiet time right now, reading, reflecting on, and writing down answers to the 25 Sacred Questions. With each question, you'll find some guidance to help spark the process of awakening your *Sacred Power of Acceptance*. There are many deeper questions we can ask ourselves beyond these 25—but this is a powerful starting point and can act as the framework for deeper exploration and the foundation for your *new* Winning Formula.

Read each question twice; then close your eyes, place your hand on your heart, and allow the answer to unfold rather than getting stuck in your head thinking about it. If you get stuck, stop, take a long, slow deep breath in, and release it as if you were purging yourself. Then go back to the process. Remember to write your answers right here in the book or keep a running journal of your responses and reflections. Whatever you choose to do, feel free to turn your contemplations into a living, breathing document in order to track your journey through your magnificent REbirth.

Carve out some quiet time for yourself before you dive into these 25 Sacred Questions. They are not meant to be answered quickly or intellectually. But rather from within, as you go deeper into your heart.

So let's begin:

1. Who am I . . . really? (Describe yourself in four sentences.)

    _____

    _____

    _____

    _____

2. Who or what is leading my life? (List the driving forces in your life that influence your behaviors, daily activities, and relationships.)

    _____

    _____

3. How do I *want* to define myself? (How do you wish you could introduce yourself to people?)

    _____

    _____

4. What do I love to do? (What activities make you smile, laugh, feel satisfied, or deeply fulfilled? What makes your heart sing when you are doing it?)

    _____

    _____

5. How can I express it on a daily basis? (List both the big and small ways that you can do what you love to do.)

_____

_____

6. What would I put on my tombstone? (At the end of your life, what will be your legacy? What value will you have added to the world? What would you like to be remembered for?)

_____

_____

7. How do I want to feel in each moment? (What are the sensations you want in your body, your heart, and your mind?)

_____

_____

8. What behaviors are feeling stale? (What actions, conditioned responses, or ways of seeing the world feel old, boring, predictable, and unfulfilling?)

_____

_____

9. How do I want to be perceived? (How do you want others describing you?)

_____

_____

10. What is really important to me now? (List your top three priorities in life.)

_____

_____

11. Who is really important to me now? (Who is rooting for you and who are you rooting for?)

_____

_____

12. How am I sacrificing what's important to me? (What are you forfeiting or compromising that matters to you?)

_____

_____

13. How am I sabotaging my successes? (What self-imposed roadblocks, unwarranted fears, and limiting beliefs are you placing in the way of your dreams?)

_____

_____

14. What are my most authentic expressions of me that I really want to be? (What are your native energies? At your core, who are you?)

_____

_____

15. What are my most inauthentic expressions of me that I don't want to be? (Where are you trying too hard? Where are you a poser?)

_____

_____

16. What are my emotional responses that are constricted? (Where do you hold back expressing yourself so you'll be perceived in a certain way? Under what circumstances are you overly reactive?)

_____

_____

17. Where am I playing small in life? (Where do you let fear drive your decision making?)

_____

_____

18. What are my emotional responses that are expanded? (Under what circumstances are you nonreactive, reflective, or creative?)

_____

_____

19. Where do I play large? (Under what circumstances are you bold, leading with love, recognizing your worthiness, and trusting the Universe?)

_____

_____

20. Who is the voice in my head when I second-guess myself? (What past or present outside influences drive you to question your decisions?)

_____

_____

21. What practices and behaviors of mine are no longer serving me? (What are your weakest daily expressions, the parts of you that just don't feel right?)

_____

_____

22. What pieces of my current winning formula are no longer serving those close to me? (How are your core relationships being negatively affected by your current Winning Formula?)

_____

_____

23. How can I begin to weave my native energies into my best expression? (List the three traits that truly define you and the best expression of them in your life.)

_____

_____

24. What is my new vision? (What is the dream you hold dear in your heart?)

_____

_____

25. What pieces of my old Winning Formula are transferable to my new vision? (List the first five action steps you will take to craft your new winning formula.)

_____

_____

As you follow this guidance, this process should start to flow pretty easily. If this is your first journey into acceptance and you are starting to feel some anxiety cropping up, do not despair! Simply reading each question out loud and silently listening for answers is a powerful step into making friends with who you are, where you've come from, and what you believe.

All the choices you made to create your old Winning Formula got you to this moment in your life. Celebrate them. Without them, you wouldn't be here. But what got you here, won't take you to the next level of your magnificence. And that's where we're headed! This process is to honor the totality of your past—the highs and lows, the peaks and valleys. Celebrate all your decisions!

THREE STEPS TO ACCEPTANCE

Seeing. If you are struggling with the concept of acceptance, take baby steps and as you ask each question, ask yourself, "What am I seeing in this situation?" Allow your full range of observation to drink in every aspect of what you perceive to be your reality. Be patient, try not to judge, and don't go beyond, "What do I see?" Simply ask over and over, "What do I see? What do I see? What do I see?" and allow answers to flow back to you.

Feeling. After you've asked and answered this question, next ask yourself, "What am I feeling in this situation?" Don't filter your emotions. Allow every possible reaction and sentiment to come into you—pain, anger, shame, guilt, happiness, pride, joy, satisfaction, excitement, nervousness, anxiousness, surprise, awe, sadness, even rage. When you feel the first wave of emotions has subsided, ask again, "What do I feel? What do I feel? What do I feel?" And allow all these feelings to flow. You may even want to write them down or come up with refined or more accurate names for your emotions.

Willingness. Tears may flow, your heart may palpitate, and a deep sense of sadness or regret may overwhelm you. This is perfect. These are simply more real emotions pouring through you—and quite honestly, they've always been there but probably have been resting in a state of sleep, denial, suppression, or disavowal. You may be skittish about the process, perhaps even fearful. And that would be natural. But next ask yourself, "What am I willing to accept?" Sit with this question, pushing it a bit further by asking, "Am I willing to accept feeling the impact on my own life without denying or judging?" And simply allow your response to bubble up. This can be a tough one. What you are really asking is, "Can I accept all the pieces of my life—the wrong turns, traumatic moments, bad choices, and their consequences, along with all the magnificence and beautiful, life-affirming decisions I've made . . . and own them all?"

Once you've become familiar with the process, I suggest you practice going deeper with your hand on your heart and your eyes closed. This is, perhaps, the most brutal inquiry of these three steps, and possibly the most challenging. In this third and final stage, you give yourself permission to truly own your life, so be gentle with yourself and take your time. Sometimes, coming face-to-face with your past can be very unsettling. But we can't release something if we don't first acknowledge that it exists! So regardless of how you feel about the past, you must accept every piece of it in order to ultimately let it go.

Once you have gone through this powerful three-step inquiry, feel free to go back and reread the 25 Sacred Questions. Remember to take long, slow, deep breaths during this process, and please take your time between each question to let the process intuitively take hold.

THE PROCESS OF TRANSFORMATION

After asking and answering the 25 Sacred Questions every day for a week, you'll begin to naturally reframe your winning formula. An internal transformation will begin to unfold, and you'll be inspired to take the following steps:

- Take out your contact lens to see what is on it.

- Take a long, slow, deep look at the road map you drafted as a child (see what have been your most conditioned responses and behaviors).

- Clean it really well by rubbing out all the distortions, lies, constrictions, and conditioned ways you've seen the world (it may be a few years since you originally crafted your Winning Formula).

- Decide what to let go of (what behaviors no longer serve you, which behaviors to make adjustments to, and which ones to reinforce).

- Set new intentions (your vision has changed).

- Evolve and recraft your new Winning Formula.

You'll want to spend some time cultivating your REbirth, so I recommend that you not feel the need to leap ahead in the book. I spent days chewing on this exercise when I began my process. Once you have gotten comfortable with your responses to the 25 Sacred Questions, you will be ready to explore the *Sacred Power of Release*.

CHAPTER SIXTEEN

THE SACRED POWER
OF RELEASE

*The day came when the risk to remain tight
in a bud was more painful than the risk it took to blossom.*

— Unknown
(common attributions: Elizabeth Appell or Anaïs Nin)

THERE ARE NO SECRETS

There is a part of you right now that needs the deepest healing—the most profound return to wholeness, the biggest shift, and that comes from beginning to release. There may be wounds, trauma, and painful memories attached to that part of you begging to be let go. And at the cellular level, every atom in your body is aware of the disturbance and suffering you have gone through and is secretly rooting for you to release it. See your whole body, mind, and Soul as fully aware of everything that has gone on and everything that needs to be done. Even if you are not fully conscious of it, there are no secrets between your heart and your soul—no mysteries or riddles that every fiber of your being does not know.

You may have innocently worked very hard to suppress your hurts and wounds, wall them off, or compartmentalize them. Yet they flow through every cell of your existence, and the pain associated with them is being felt throughout your body even when your attention isn't on them. They can flare up in an instant by having the right hot button pushed or tender spot being touched.

Before you let go, you must loosen your grip. And this is most easily done when we give ourselves permission to do the following:

Begin the process.

Own our impact.

Let go of what no longer serves us.

Step into a new beginning.

> *"We all need to visit the land of hurts and wounds once in a while, but no one needs to live there."*

Loosening Your Grip

Before taking a step toward REbirth, many people struggle with constricted outlooks, conditioned internal conversations, peer-pressured viewpoints, uninspired attitudes, and hand-me-down belief systems. Remind yourself as you walk through this process of REbirth that part of you will boldly step out of the shadows and into the light. Are you ready to do that right now? If that sounds scary, then simply dip your toe in. Let's begin to awaken your *Sacred Power of Release* by gently giving yourself permission to move forward. Answer this question right now:

Am I ready and willing to awaken the sacred power of REbirth in my life right now?

If you are not sure, do not despair. It just means that you are still very tender. Regardless of your answer, here's another set of questions that you can answer to help you gain clarity and perspective.

On a scale of 1 to 10, where 1 is not at all, and 10 is extremely, answer these three questions:

1. *How badly do I need a second chance?*

2. *How deeply do I desire a fresh start?*

3. *How worthy do I feel I am for a new beginning?*

If your total score is 15 or higher, you are ready to move forward. If your combined score is less than 15, then simply identify one aspect of your life that could use a fresh start; and ask the questions about this aspect of your life. Sometimes getting really specific helps to spark our permission center.

Whatever your score was, we can awaken your *Sacred Power of Release* with an ancient energetic process referred to as the YUM HAAM Meditation.

Simply follow along with this meditation, and soon we'll all be on the same page. As you heal throughout the remaining exercises and teachings of the Sacred Powers, you will accelerate your confidence and spark your REbirth.

Awakening Forgiveness and Permission Meditation

The ancient teachings of energetic flow say that your heart is your forgiveness center and your throat is your permission center. To awaken your power of REbirth, we need to awaken forgiveness and permission, forgive ourselves for everything that's ever happened in our lives, and grant our self-permission to heal, move forward, and thrive. First, find a comfortable space to sit or lay down. Place your left hand on your heart, and rest your right hand against your throat.

We'll spend just a few minutes on this meditation. As you breathe in, feel your left hand on your heart rise up with your expanded chest. Silently repeat, *I forgive myself.* As you exhale, feel the breath under your right hand move through your throat, and silently repeat, *I give myself permission to begin again.*

Get into a rhythmic flow as you practice this five times; then close your eyes and continue for a few minutes. I'll wait right here.

The Ancient Practice

Welcome back. Feels pretty liberating. Right? A sense of calm and empowerment should be blanketing you right now, so let's take our REbirth even deeper. Keeping your hands where they were, instead of repeating, *I forgive myself* as you inhale, silently whisper, *YUM*, the ancient Sanskrit vibration of the heart chakra (where forgiveness rests). And instead of repeating, *I give myself permission to begin again,* as you exhale, silently whisper, *HAAM*, the ancient Sanskrit vibration of the throat chakra (where permission rests). Breathe in and silently repeat YUM; breathe out and silently repeat HAAM. *YUM HAAM . . . YUM HAAM . . . YUM HAAM.* And now continue on for another few minutes with your eyes closed.

You can use the English version or the ancient Sanskrit version of the YUM HAAM. It's totally up to you. Both will have powerful results. And, whenever you start to drift into your old Winning Formula, use these tools to help you awaken the *Sacred Power of Release*. Feeling lighter? Let's keep going.

RITUAL + MEANING = TRANSFORMATION

The ritual of initiation—either by fire or in a body of water—is essentially a REbirth, a letting go of what no longer serves, combined with the awakening of an inward grace. Cleansing. Releasing. Awakening.

These practices have been around in some form or another for more than 5,000 years and had their first start in the earliest cradles of civilization in Asia, the Middle East, Africa, and the

Americas. They've been practiced throughout time by the Vikings of Scandinavia, the Mayans of Mexico, Native and First Nation cultures in the Americas, and in the more formalized religions of Hinduism, Buddhism, Taoism, Christianity, Judaism, and Islam.

Water Is the Cleanse

Water has often been used in these ceremonies as a vehicle of cleansing to reconnect the initiate to the Universal journey each of us experiences. By stepping out of the sacred waters of our mother's nourishing womb and then washing away the blood, placenta, and amniotic fluid of our past, our divine purity, untainted heart, and unstained soul resting within are revealed.

Fire Is the Release

The unrelenting, all-consuming nature of fire has always signified the personal transformation we experience as we step from one chapter of our life and into the next. The *ritualized burning away of the past* in a bonfire and the steaming away of limiting beliefs in a native sweat lodge or Mayan *Temazcal* are 1,000-year-old initiations based on the capacity of fire to incinerate, obliterate, and transform everything it touches. These rituals indelibly imprint themselves on our subconscious with the force to eradicate a conditioned, patterned behavior. Because once a possibility has been turned to dust, the seeds of a new possibility are then free to plant themselves in fertile soil. This is the opportunity for the phoenix to rise up from the ashes.

The Sacred Fire Ritual of Release and REbirth

I often integrate water and fire ceremonies into my retreats and teacher trainings to ritualize the letting go of what no longer serves us and celebrate the transformational initiation of REbirth into more expanded horizons. Ritualizing any practice gives it energy, and adding meaning to that ritual takes it to an evolutionary place of pure potential. Ritual + meaning = transformation.

So right now, let's perform a sacred fire release ritual that will have immediate effects. You can do this in a sacred private ceremony all by yourself, or you can invite others to participate, so you can all feed off the collective energy. If there will be others, feel free to guide them all through the process.

First you'll need to find or build a fire. If you have access to the outdoors, build a small bonfire, turn on a fire pit, or simply light the barbecue. If you have a fireplace, get it cooking. Otherwise, find a fireproof receptacle that can serve as your mini–fire pit, such as an ashtray or a Pyrex bowl. Don't use your sink or tub, anything made of plastic, or anything flammable. And just in case, fill a pot or a bucket with water, so you can quickly douse it if the flames get out of hand. Next:

Get a pen or marker and a piece of paper, and write down three things you would like to let go of in your life. Don't type it; write them down using ink or marker. They can be big things or tiny things. It could be the big dream that is just not going to happen but is preventing you from dreaming a new dream. Maybe it's a habit or non-nourishing behavior; maybe it's a perspective or a way you see the world; maybe it's a physical object like clothes that don't fit or a box you've been clinging to; maybe it's a relationship or the way you feel about a person. Simply write down whatever it is and be specific. Then crumple up the piece of paper, hold it tightly in your hand, and rest your hand against your heart. As you hold the paper to your chest, allow any constriction, emotional charge, toxicity, or turbulence you feel inside to move around.

Connect to the sadness, frustration, irritation, anger, grievance, resentment, outrage, or disappointment you feel right now in this moment and allow those emotions to stir. Once they are mobilized, watch them move from inside your heart outward toward your hand and into the crumpled paper. Witness the emotions as they leave your heart and flow into the paper. Feel the sensation of your heart emptying these destructive emotions.

Feel them moving past your fingertips into that crumpled paper in your hand. And now stay in this space for five minutes with your eyes closed, letting all the negative energy in your cells leave your body and move into the paper. I'll sit right here and wait with you . . .

If you're reading this, it means you've completed the first part of the ritual. So now let's move to the second part—the fire part. Your paper is fully charged; your heart is a bit lighter.

Now say a prayer of release or letting go such as:

"There was a time when I thought you were important to me. That time has come and gone. Right now, I ask for the courage and the strength to let you go from my life. With the support of the Universe, I release you."

Toss your piece of paper into the bonfire, firepit, barbecue, or fireplace, or light the paper and place it into the receptacle you've chosen. This is the important part: Make sure to watch the flames entirely consume your piece of paper charged with all that negative energy. Then place your hands on your tender heart, and with your eyes closed, just softly breathe, as you witness the last pieces of negative energy leave your body. Throughout the process, feel free to chant, hum, sing, whisper, or speak whatever comes to mind. Stay in this sacred space until the paper has turned to ash and until all the flames have been reduced to embers. If you've done this indoors, feel free to add to the ritual by flushing the ashes down the toilet.

When I perform this ritual, as the paper is burning, I like to repeat the first three words of the Rig Veda, the oldest book in existence: *Agni meele purohitam* (pronounced ahg-nee mee-lay pooroh-heetam), which means "I surrender to the fire of transformation!" Chanting this over and over helps me connect to the 5,000-year-old cosmic stream of ancient ritual and release.

Full Release Ritual

There's another ritual that can amplify your release and really increase the cathartic aspects of the process. I live near the beach, and if you live near the ocean or have access to any body of water, you can take this ritual to the next level. First, find a rock that you can hold comfortably in your hand. Just like we did with the piece of paper, use a Sharpie and write down on the rock the thing you most want to let go of. Once you've defined that rock, hold it close to your heart and let all that darkness leave your body and flow right into the rock. Continuing to hold them tightly to your heart, charge both the rock and the paper with your emotional pain. Let all your anger, sadness, regret, rage, and bitterness release from your body and move into the rock and the piece of paper.

Maintaining silence the whole time, make your way to the body of water. At the edge of the water, wind up and hurl your rock into the water. As you let go, scream a deep release howl, yelling anything that will ritualize the process, such as, "I'm done with you!" "I release you!" "You don't own me anymore!" "AAAAH-HHH!" "I set you free!" "F*#@ you!" or any expression that feels right in the moment. It's also very healthy to say a person's name who is attached to your pain or suffering. It helps release them from your heart. Spend a few minutes feeling the release after that part of the ritual. Then proceed to the place of your sacred fire ceremony and fully surrender to the fire of transformation, where you will watch the paper burn and its contents turn to ash.

Nature Abhors a Vacuum

The hours, days, and weeks following this ritual will have a special flavor to them. There will be a lightness of being that follows you everywhere. You will breathe more easily and your heart will feel a bit more relaxed. But most important, you will have created some space inside. This will spark the energetic movement that will invite new, fresh, expansiveness into your life.

The ancient Greek philosopher Aristotle taught that nature abhors a vacuum, meaning that the Universal laws of science and physics require every space be filled with something. Now that the emotional charge that once filled your heart has been released and the energetic toxicity in each of your cells has dissipated, there is room for something new, unconditioned, undefined, and limitless. If darkness has left, there is room for light; if suffering has left, there is room for relief. If sadness has left, there is room for joy. If pain has left, there is room for soothing.

This is the truest expression of the *Sacred Power of Release*, a divine magnetism that pulls newness into emptiness!

CHAPTER SEVENTEEN

THE SACRED POWER
OF NEW BEGINNINGS

Every day I feel is a blessing from God.
And I consider it a new beginning.
Yeah, everything is beautiful.

— Prince

RETURNING TO WHOLENESS

At the moment you were born, you were perfect, pure, and whole. You were so innocent, so accepting, and you had a beginner's mind regarding all things. You were curious as you slowly discovered the world around you. All of your words and actions came from a place of vulnerability and defenselessness. Every experience was as if it were the first time. You moved through each moment with pure acceptance, as if you had never known the sting of harm, shame, guilt, or grievance, and knew only the sweetness, goodness, and kind flow of the Universe.

But then you began to resist certain things. You started to choose. You started to judge. And your acceptance became less unconditional. And since then, over the years, you have resisted quite a few things. You've crossed your arms to block acceptance many times. But the time for resistance is over! It's time to reconnect to that beginner's mind. Time to reawaken our innocence and curiosity about what life could now offer us. The Universe only wants to elevate you, celebrate you, cradle you lovingly in its divine arms, and gift you with a fresh start. When we awaken the *Sacred Power of New Beginnings*, we open ourselves back up to that innocence and acceptance, which is the seed of our REbirth.

WORTHY OF A NEW BEGINNING

We know that whatever choices we've made, we made them from our highest level of consciousness at the time. But in some cases, a lack of purpose has guided those decisions. In fact, there may be many steps you've taken where if you could choose them differently right now, you would. If you have regrets over things you've said and done, or choices you've made that you wish you could take back, you are not alone.

So many people *live in eternal pain*, because they are incapable of forgiving themselves; many *are afraid to follow their hearts*, because they can't bear the pain of it breaking again; others *question their self-worth*, because they are convinced God or the Universe does not love them unconditionally, and they *won't forgive themselves*, because they don't believe they are entitled to be free from the karma of their actions. Here's the reality: good people can make bad choices. And bad choices don't make a bad person. The late, great Sufi Master and sage David Simon taught me that if you are willing to wholeheartedly own and accept a choice you've made, *defenselessly* without making any excuses, *and* if you believe in your heart of hearts that with everything you now know you would make a different choice today in that same situation, then you are worthy of forgiveness and entitled to forgive yourself.

The *Divine Principle of REbirth* teaches that there is redemption in every moment if you are willing to own your impact, forgive yourself, and make a more conscious choice. The *Sacred Power of New Beginnings* is your permission slip to take a fresh, new, bold step on the Divine Path of REbirth.

We are more aware now than we were as children. We have the experience and ability to derive more of our self-worth from our own self rather than from others. But we have conditioned and reinforced our less attractive traits over and over every day for decades. We've conditioned and reinforced our more attractive traits as well. The *New Beginnings Blueprint* is a powerful tool to help you reflect on your decisions, better understand their consequences, and make new, purposeful, nourishing choices going forward.

It contains only seven questions, but they require total, pure, raw honesty. Completing this part of the process will act as your formal initiation into REbirth. Begin to write the answers to these questions. Your responses can be as brief as a few sentences or as deep as 30 pages. It may even become the outline for your next book! As you proceed, you will witness your new beginning unfolding. So allow the process to flow with innocence, and trust that you are moving toward transformation.

The New Beginnings Blueprint

Use these seven core questions to outline your REbirth blueprint:

1. What has been my Winning Formula?
2. When and why did I create it?
3. What has it brought me?
4. What has it cost me?
5. What is my true vision?
6. What are the five steps I can take to move me from where I am to where I want to be?
7. What is the commitment I make right now?

Note for the high achiever: speed is not the goal. Clarity is critical. We all can bang out answers in a few minutes, but that would be the old Winning Formula taking over. Reel it back in. We are making a powerful shift and undoing decades of conditioning, so take it slow and easy. Asking and answering these questions may take time. Be patient, but begin now and as the days unfold, you will have your new blueprint developed. You will have begun the process of REbirth!

After Clarity . . . Commitment

Question seven asks, "What is the commitment I make right now?" Commitments are sacred contracts that we make with our souls. They are the divine agreements that transcend space and time. They are the foundations of our *New Beginnings*, because they are pure and carry with them the best of intentions. Embedded in every commitment is the most devotional desire to transform in some way. The ancient Indian text, the Brihadaranyaka Upanishad, guides us with the phrase: "You are your deepest driving desire. As is your desire, so is your will. As is your will, so is your deed. As is your deed, so is your destiny." Our desire to transform is the seed that sparks the process. And then our commitment helps us to lean in the direction of the dream. Our commitment sits at the very edge of transformation. When we push that edge, energy begins to move creating the path to our REbirth.

INNOCENCE + COMMITMENT

Once the energy of the *Sacred Powers of Acceptance*, *Release*, and *New Beginnings* are awakened, we experience the fusion of the openhearted defenselessness of our childhood innocence with the deep, driving commitment embedded in our heart. From this merging, REbirth becomes a self-fulfilling prophecy. It sparks a transformation that can only end in the actualization of your new vision, the logical fulfillment of your intention, and the full realization of your deep dream. REbirth is our birthright. We are worthy in every moment of being reborn. And, through awakening these three Sacred Powers, the momentum of our transformation picks up speed.

Slide over into the passenger seat and let the Universe take the wheel.

BEGINNING AGAIN

We cultivate our *Sacred Power of New Beginnings* through a series of transformational rituals—five powerful daily practices that can be used individually or in combination. Each practice offers you an opportunity to cultivate renewal, a fresh start, or a new beginning. All five practiced on a daily basis will nourish your REbirth:

1. Asking the Four Sacred Questions of REbirth

2. The New Beginnings Meditation

3. The Sacred Affirmation of REbirth

4. Performing the Sacred Rite of New Beginnings

5. Taking Your Action Step

When we first sit down for our morning ritual, we begin by asking ourselves a series of Sacred Questions. These four questions are designed to spark a dialogue between you and the Universe. We close our eyes, place our hands over our hearts, and silently ask each question. Sometimes answers will flow. Sometimes there will be no answers. It's very common for answers to come back to you hours or days later. The key is to ask the Sacred Questions over and over until they become part of your inner dialogue. In time they will become part of your outer dialogue as well. And this is how energy effortlessly transforms from questions to awakenings to answers to choices to actions to REbirth.

Every Day Is a New Day

To activate the *Sacred Power of New Beginnings* at the start of your day, find a comfortable place to sit or lie down, even if it's just for a few minutes. Take the time to just *be*. I can't stress the importance of this enough. It ends up creating a brand-new trajectory of everything the follows in your day. If you start your day in turmoil, then that is what will follow you all day long. Those same hormones and chemicals that were infused into you in the morning will continue to surge into you over the course of the day. And if you start your day with a little bit of stillness, then patience, calm, and clarity will set the tone for a new beginning.

Once you are settled into a comfortable position, place your hands on your heart, and begin the practice of asking the Sacred Questions. Simply ask the first question over and over for about a minute, then the second question, then the third, and then the fourth, always waiting for answers to unfold without forcing. Feel free to spend up to a minute with each question. When you have completed the process, take a long, slow, deep breath in and release all the questions and any answers that arose. Then invite an intention into your mind regarding one aspect of your life you desire to REbirth. Get clear on it, invite it into your heart, and plant that intention like a seed in the fertile soil of your heart. Then breathe in deeply, and let it go. Leave it up to the Universe to work out all the details. Then begin your meditation practice.

The Four Sacred Questions for REbirth

To reclaim ownership of your life through acceptance, grant yourself the permission to release what no longer serves you, and boldly step into new beginnings, start the practice by asking the *Four Sacred Questions of REbirth*:

1. Who am I when I'm at my best?
2. What can I let go of that no longer serves me?
3. Do I give myself permission right now to step into my power of new beginnings?
4. What step can I take today to awaken my best version?

The New Beginnings Meditation

After we've asked and answered the sacred questions and let go of any outcomes, we are ready to take the process even deeper. Remember, in every meditation, comfort is queen, so keep moving toward comfort. And just as we practiced in the YUM HAAM Meditation, place your left hand on your heart and rest your right hand against your throat.

Now simply witness. Patiently watch your breathing and your body for a few moments. As you breathe in, feel your left hand on your heart rise up with your expanded chest and silently repeat, *Today*. As you exhale, feel the breath under your right hand move out through your throat, and silently repeat, *I begin*. Continue to slowly breathe, silently repeating, *Today* as you inhale and *I begin* as you exhale. *Today . . . I begin*. You'll start to feel the words have a vibration that moves in and out through you as you breathe. There is no correct speed; simply surrender to the process and go wherever it takes you.

Get into a rhythmic flow as you practice five inhales and exhales. Then close your eyes and continue for a few minutes, or as long as feels comfortable up to 30 minutes. If you start your morning with this powerful meditation, this powerful mantra will ripple through you all day long and you will feel new beginnings take hold, starting with your very first conversations and activities of the day.

Starting your day with a meditation ritual provides the perfect environment for your daily REbirth to begin and for your day to unfold with greater grace and greater ease. When we begin our day in stillness and silence, we are connected to source and that then becomes the trajectory of every other moment. We have a seed pregnant with possibilities—a seed that has its manifestation already built in being planted into a vibrationally fertile environment that will help it thrive. And from there, our REbirth flows.

THE SACRED AFFIRMATION OF REBIRTH

The Sacred Affirmation builds on the mantra you used in the meditation, reinforcing and reminding you to see with new eyes. We've already discussed how powerful affirmations can be in those moments of questioning whether we are on the right path. This affirmation is a Universal truth; it cuts through doubt, our moments of wavering faith, and our natural inclination to second-guess our self. The Sacred Affirmation of REbirth is:

With every breath, I am REborn. Today I begin again.

Imagine how you will feel when these are the very first words you utter as you begin your day. Feel free to repeat the Sacred Affirmation whenever you sense you are giving your power away, holding on to something that doesn't serve you, or doubting your worthiness for a second chance.

We can also repeat the affirmation at a regularly scheduled interval such as every hour or two hours starting at 8 A.M. I recommend that you use the affirmation as a reinforcement tool right before you open any door, whether it is for a room, building, or vehicle. By ritualizing the Sacred Affirmation, you ingrain the concept of REbirth into every thought, word, and action, and awaken your ability to accept the moment, release what no longer serves you, and embrace a new beginning.

THE SACRED MANTRA

When we explored the *Sacred Power of Acceptance*, we learned how a mantra can effortlessly transport us out of the past and future and deliver us to the present moment. Repeating a mantra can cut through the swirl of activity in our mind and connect us to a still point of unconditioned thought. This is particularly powerful in those moments where a break from conditioned thought patterns is just what's needed to allow us to step into a new idea, a fresh perspective, or a new belief system. We can accelerate the awakening of our *Sacred Power of New Beginnings* by practicing a Universal mantra that combines an ancient Sanskrit vibration and its English translation. This transformational mantra is:

MOKSHA (pronounced moke-sha). I am free.

Moksha (pronounced moke-sha) is a concept that was first discussed 2,500 years ago in the ancient Vedic text the Katha Upanishad, where it referred to one's emancipation from the ongoing cycle of birth, death, and rebirth. But for thousands of years, it was also defined as our perfect state of being, a pure liberation, where we are fully released from our ego and all the emotional constrictions that weigh so heavily on us. I define moksha in the real-world sense of being totally free from the past. However you define it, know that it comes from the Sanskrit root *muc*, which means free, let go, or release.

You can silently whisper it to yourself during your Sacred Rite; repeat it out loud while you are commuting to work; or simply use it as a pattern interruption whenever you find yourself slipping into an old, constricted pattern or a non-nourishing behavior. When the world feels like it's closing in on you or you feel like you've come to a dead end, simply bring yourself back to, *Moksha. I am free.*

Side note: my second album of guided meditations, *Journey to Infinity*, with the Canadian sound-healing duo Sacred Fire, includes a transformational track called "Moksha," which continues to be one of the most powerful meditations I've ever recorded. If you'd like to use this meditation as part of your REbirth practice, send me an e-mail (info@davidji.com) and I'll send you the file for your music library.

PERFORMING THE SACRED RITE OF NEW BEGINNINGS

We've asked the Sacred Questions, set the stage for REbirth through meditation, repeated the Sacred Affirmation, and now it's time to connect your physical body to your heart and mind. This fusion of physical, emotional, mental, and spiritual energy is referred to as the *Sacred Rite of New Beginnings*.

Stand up, feet shoulder width apart. Place your palms together and bring them to your heart. Gaze up to the sky and envision all the stardust in the Universe raining down on you. Close your eyes. And take a long, slow, deep breath in as you lower yourself into a squat.

Now leap up from your crouch, raising your hands to the sky, as you repeat the following mantra out loud:

MOKSHA! Today, I begin again.

It may seem silly at first, but by adding this physical activity to your integrated process, you will turn thoughts into action. Furthermore, you will engrain the physical act of REbirth into your awareness. You will feel it in every fiber of your being. Throughout the day, as you bump into obstacles, realize you are playing small, or begin to compromise your Sacred Values, use the memory of you standing, crouching down, and leaping up to reinforce your new decisions, new directions, and newfound ability to REbirth. Then whisper, "MOKSHA! Today I begin again."

When it comes to REbirth, remember:

1. You are never stuck; the Universe has decreed that you are worthy of REbirth.

2. You always have the power within to shift your life from where you are to where you'd like to be.

3. Change is different than transformation. Change is finite; transformation is evolution.

4. The Winning Formula of your life has gotten you to this point; your new Winning Formula will take you to the next level.

5. You can REbirth any moment by accepting what is, releasing what no longer serves you, and stepping into a new beginning.

Here we are in this sacred, precious present moment. What are you going to do with it?

The Fourth Secret

THE DIVINE
PRINCIPLE OF
INFINITE FLOW

The Divine Principle of Infinite Flow
and
the Sacred Powers of
Trust, Abundance, and Shakti

CHAPTER EIGHTEEN

WALKING THE FOURTH DIVINE PATH

Letting the Universe In

To see a World in a Grain of Sand
And a Heaven in a Wild Flower
Hold Infinity in the palm of your hand
And Eternity in an hour.

— William Blake

THE ENERGY OF THE UNIVERSE IS RESTING IN YOUR SOUL

We are beings of dynamic, energetic exchange. The wind becomes our breath, which becomes the oxygen that nourishes the blood flowing through our cells that trigger chemicals that impact your nerves, which spark electrical impulses that move your eyeballs and let you read these words. And then you exhale, releasing carbon dioxide into the world, nourishing plants and trees that soak up water from the earth and the sky. In each moment, the cycle continues through every single cell on the planet, effortlessly allowing nourishment to flow into them, in turn, generously offering back out what they do not need. This divine life force flows through everything leaving magnificent transformation in its wake.

The most fundamental law of nature is that energy cannot be created or destroyed. In every millisecond, you and me—and the whole planet—are simply continuing a flow of cosmic energy that began billions of years ago. Our entire existence in this lifetime is built on the premise of a never-ending energy exchange, which has been known for millennia as the *Divine Principle of Infinite Flow*. It ripples through everything, in every moment, without beginning or end. It ripples through me and through you. It's rippling right now. It was never born and has never died. It is pure unbounded circulation.

If you've ever wondered, "Am I breathing in the Universe? Or is the Universe breathing me?" the answer is actually a little bit of both. We call this experience one of *dynamic exchange*. In fact, every heartbeat, every sound you hear, every word you speak, every sensation you feel is one of *dynamic exchange*. The best example of this phenomenon is when you hug someone. You lean in and wrap your arms around them. They wrap their arms around you, and, in an instant, you are both the hugger and the huggee. Each of you is acting as an energetic conduit, flowing attention, affection, appreciation, and acceptance to and from each other, all in just a few seconds.

Now imagine a hug that has been going on since before time began—a hug between every single aspect of the Universe, one with no end in sight. This uninterrupted, reciprocal, endless passing back and forth of energy is the hallmark of the *Divine Principle of Infinite Flow*.

THE ETERNAL RIVER

Through much of our life, we've been brainwashed to see ourselves as physical beings having the occasional spiritual experience. That's why this existence of ours can feel so challenging in certain moments. But walking this Fourth Divine Path guides us to a deeper truth that negates the brainwashing and teaches instead that you and I are magnificent energetic expressions of the Divine who happen to be sealed in these individual flesh casings for the span of a lifetime. Thousands of years ago, the teachers of ancient wisdom traditions reinforced this understanding by revealing that we are in fact spiritual beings having this momentary physical experience—

that our bodily existence is like a flash of lightning in the night sky. And that is why modern-day astronomer, cosmologist, and astrophysicist Carl Sagan wrote, "We are like butterflies who flutter for a day and think it is forever." But if we go deeper, beneath this physical body, beneath our ego, beneath our conditioning, beneath our thoughts, and go deeper still, we discover that we are simply singular expressions of this divine collective cosmic flow, circulating pure energy like an eternal river.

A HOLE IN THE FLUTE

This *Divine Principle of Infinite Flow* is an eternal Law of the Universe that has been celebrated on earth for more than 5,000 years by the oldest of civilizations. This timeless principle was depicted in hieroglyphics on early Egyptian pyramid walls and referenced in the ancient scriptures of the Old Testament, the Bhagavad Gita, and the Tao Te Ching. You and I are simply conduits of energy—letting it in and flowing it back out. One of the most beautiful descriptions of the *Divine Principle of Infinite Flow* was portrayed by the 12th century Sufi poet Hafiz, when he wrote, "I am a hole in the flute through which the Christ breath flows." We are simply empty spaces, channels, infinite threads in the eternal fabric of existence. We're not the flute, not the breath, not Christ. We are simply the hole, a divine conduit for energy to pass through us.

The wind blows and we breathe in. The Universe flickers and our mind sparks. Then a thought is birthed, a word is spoken, or an action is taken. And the ripples of energy gain velocity as our eyes, voices, and vibrations touch others, get translated, reinterpreted, ingested, and absorbed. Their essence is passed on in an endless game of tag, redigested, re-metabolized, and shared in words, actions, and energy by an exponentially larger group in an infinite global contagion that transcends the boundaries of our existence as we know it.

This convergence of infinite flow and dynamic exchange makes up all the interactions on the planet, from the warmth of the sun heating and fueling all life on earth to someone feeling cold and closing a window. The relentless flow of existence goes on forever in a cosmic dance of dynamic exchange.

YOU ARE A LIVING, BREATHING TRANSFORMATION MACHINE!

Take a deep breath in right now. 78 percent of that breath is nitrogen, 21 percent is oxygen, a little less than 1 percent is argon, and the remaining two-fifths of 1 percent is a tiny mixture of carbon dioxide and water vapor. Who knew? When you exhale, your breath contains the exact same percentage of nitrogen and argon you inhaled. You hold on to none of it because it doesn't serve you. But you do hold on to one-fourth of the oxygen you inhaled, and it merges with your blood to nourish your organs and sustain life in your body. We release only 16 percent of the pure oxygen we ingested back out into the air. The remaining oxygen we inhaled is mixed with the carbon in our body to create a massive amount of carbon dioxide, which then gets exhaled back out into the air mixed with some water vapor. Essentially, every breath you take holds on to 25 percent of the oxygen you inhale and releases 100 times the amount of carbon dioxide you inhale. As we breathe, approximately 20,000 times a day, we are subtly transforming our bodies, our cellular structure, our environment, and the planet.

Human beings are beings of dynamic flow. We access the world through our senses, physically and emotionally *ingest* it, and then *digest* it with our bodies and our minds. Ideally, we absorb what we believe will serve us, integrate it into our being, and release the non-nourishing aspects. As we've seen, this transformation process is most obvious with the air we breathe, but we also do this on a grand emotional scale.

JUST ANOTHER STOP IN THE COSMIC FLOW

Once we have tasted, broken down, and digested our thoughts, conversations, and interactions, we pass them through our unique filter of conditioning, where our memories, beliefs, attitudes, and perspectives merge with our needs, desires, and dreams. We then flow them back out into the world in a powerful expression of transformation as we turn idea into action, thought into word, and concept into reality. We've observed it in the corporate world as the spark of an idea became a product—a texting device, which morphed into the mobile phone, which then added a camera, and then apps, which then transformed our ability to use social media platforms, such as Facebook, Twitter, and Instagram, which in turn touch billions of people every day, influencing behavior, culture, and life choices in every corner of the world, impacting relationships, careers, education, commerce, recreation, elections, policy decisions, the pace of change, and global transformation in virtually every aspect of existence. And we see that same ripple in ourselves as a thought flickers into our awareness and sparks us to take action that touches another person, who then responds with a series of their own thoughts, actions, and interactions. And it's never ending.

The *Divine Principle of Infinite Flow* has existed for eternity. Those who have embraced it, mastered it, and leveraged it have achieved the highest levels of personal and professional success. Three sacred powers rest at the foundation of this timeless truth of circulation since humankind first walked the earth:

The Sacred Power of Trust

The Sacred Power of Abundance

The Sacred Power of Shakti

Awakening these powers aligns you more closely with the Universe, releases all constrictions and resistance, and accelerates the *Divine Principle of Infinite Flow* in your life.

153

CHAPTER NINETEEN

THE SACRED POWER
OF TRUST

To have faith is to trust yourself to the water.
When you swim you don't grab hold of the water,
because if you do you will sink and drown.
Instead you relax, and float.

— Alan Watts

THE MEANING OF TRUST

You are already connected to everything you could ever desire or need right now, but you must trust to receive them. *What's trust?* The breath you're taking right now; the next thought that drifts into your awareness; your body's constant questing for balance; the trillions of vibrations rippling through every aspect of your being; listening to the tender feelings in your heart; the sensations in your flesh; energy flowing through your mind and heart; the digestion of your physical and emotional experiences; and, your ability to transform this moment into the next.

Trust is a Sacred Power; it requires no convincing. Trust is having a firm belief that whatever is flowing through you, flows through everything. It has been flowing through the cosmos for billions of years and will continue to flow for all eternity. Trust is deeply embedded at your very core. You can't think your way into trust. You can't intellectualize it. Trust only ripens when you are ready.

TRUST IS AN INVITATION

In every moment that you trust, you are inviting the magnificence of the Universe into your life with unwavering confidence. And when you lose faith, it's not as if you have suddenly found someone else to invite. No. You haven't rested your trust in some *other* magnificence or some *other* divine principle. In that moment of wavering, you question inviting *anyone* or *anything* into your life. When you stop trusting, you suddenly lose confidence in your decision. You mistakenly believe that you know better than the Universe, and you unconsciously stop believing in the *Divine Principle of Infinite Flow*. You selectively turn your back on the laws of the Universe and on everything you truly know to be true, like suddenly not believing that gravity will hold you down or that electricity will work when you flick on the light.

When you stop trusting, you suspend reality, disconnect from the effortless support of the Universe, and inexplicably choose to proceed with no divine support. As the Father of Motivation, Dr. Wayne Dyer, shared with me before his passing, "When you stop trusting, you let your *EGO* take over. You *E*dge *G*od *O*ut."

Trust is when you are fully aligned with the Universe in thought, breath, word, and deed. When you are in that alignment, you allow the magnificence inside of you to shine and yourself to step out of the way. It's as if the Universe is holding your hand and walking right beside you. Those are the moments of spontaneous right speech, where every word you say fits perfectly into the moment and accomplishes your short-term, long-term, and other people's goals simultaneously. Clarity unfolds perfectly. Sometimes we call this "being in the zone" or having a "win-win" experience. In this moment of pure present moment awareness, every intention you have, every choice you make, every action you take fits into the situation perfectly. It feels really good *and* it serves the Universe.

As long as we stay open and trusting, everything that's meant to move through us comes in effortlessly, *and* flows back out with grace. Openness is the key. As long as the conduit is wide open, the whole process will be organic and fluid. But the moment we put up barriers, get defensive, or question whether we should receive the flow, *boom!*, the flow narrows or stops altogether and the trust is broken.

FEAR OR TRUST

So what gets in the way? What creates the constriction? The culprit is *fear*, the emotion we feel when we sense a threat. When we sense a physical threat, fear usually expresses itself through a primitive biological response mechanism known as fight-flight, which helps us fight or run from a situation to protect ourselves. When our lives are not in danger, but we sense a threat to our beliefs, opinions, or expectations, the exact same biological response mechanism inspires us to emotionally fight or flee using words or body language. We forget the *Divine Principle of Infinite Flow*. We stop trusting that every moment is perfect and that all is progressing as it was divinely intended. We begin to micromanage the Universe and express ourselves by constricting, defending, or resisting.

Practicing defenselessness is a way to transcend the fear and realign with trust.

LACK OF TRUST = FEAR

Fear has often been explained as F.E.A.R.: False. Evidence. Appearing. Real. Fear is simply a false projection of what the future may hold. A bad guess. A negative wish. It's that hiccup in the present moment where we stop trusting the Universe, suspending all we know to be true, and instead start believing in *false evidence*. And yet we hold our fears to be as real as the reality of this moment. They freeze us. They frighten us. They hold us back from moving forward. They hold us in this fantasy world where we believe that what we've made up in our mind will indeed come to pass. And, these self-created fantasies are as real to us as anything that's actually ever happened.

But they are the darkest pieces of our imagination. They are the inventions of the part of us that does not trust. And in our chronic lack of trust, we repeat our fears like affirmations over and over in our mind until they harden like concrete. And even though these projections most likely will never come to pass, we hold on to them with deep faith, so that if they do happen, we prove ourselves right in a heartbreaking, self-fulfilling prophecy. And, of course, if they end up not coming true, we rarely stop and celebrate. Rather, we become so transfixed on *the negative scenario that didn't happen* that we are blind to the beauty that actually does unfold.

Fear obscures the opportunity that sits right before us. Fear colors every thought that has the potential to sprout into magnificence. As the Buddha said, "All that we are arises with our thoughts. With our thoughts, we create our world." And when we convince ourselves that what we want to happen won't and what we don't want to happen will, then we become a victim of our dumbed-down, constricted, conditioned versions of ourselves.

But we are better than that. We are stronger than that. We are more capable and blessed than we often give ourselves credit for. *When we surrender to fear, it is because we don't trust.* When we buy into fear, in that moment, we are not trusting the Divine, not trusting our choices, not trusting ourselves to make right decisions, and not trusting that there is a much bigger picture, one that takes into account all the moving parts of the Universe. When we come from fear, there is a struggle within each of us where the worst possible scenario battles the best possible scenario for attention.

Living Trust

And so, when we find ourselves questioning our judgment . . . when we hear the voice in our head telling us we are less-than or not worthy, we need to know that the word *trust* can be reconfigured into *strut!* And that's how we activate the *Sacred Power of Trust.* By giving yourself permission to strut, to believe again and open your heart to the possibility that whatever negativity you can dream up is *False Evidence Appearing Real* and can easily be offset by a positive internal conversation.

We must remind ourselves that we have a choice in each moment, and that we can choose the best outcome or the most painful outcome. When we make the choice from a place of detachment—trusting that we are not alone and that the Universe is in control—then the highest choice wins!

One of the most powerful tools in creating trust in your life is accepting that trusting what's best for the Universe will ultimately be best for you. That's the *Sacred Power of Trust* in a nutshell. The *Divine Principle of Infinite Flow* is your birthright. You are whole, and pure, and perfect, and infinite—evolving in every single moment toward a magnificent, ideal version of yourself. Sometimes we need a kick-start to remind us of our true, eternal, and boundless nature so that we can truly see infinite possibilities in moments of thinking small, feeling stuck, or buying into limiting beliefs. We can access our unbounded view of existence through a simple practice known as Infinity Breath.

Find a place where you can sit or lie down, and get as comfortable as possible. Gently take long, slow, silent breaths in and out through your nostrils. If you are hearing the air move through your nose, you are moving too quickly. Slowly draw the divine breath of the Universe deeply into you, gently expanding your belly. When it reaches its fullest point, slowly and silently allow the air inside to effortlessly flow back out of your nose. Continue this practice 10 times until you actually feel yourself slowing down.

Now take it further by allowing the inhale to flow seamlessly into the exhale and the exhale to flow seamlessly back into the inhale, without any pause between. Turn it into a flow. At the end of each inhale, gently, silently turn the breath around and release it back out. At the end of each exhale, quietly turn the breath around and begin to draw breath back in through your nose.

Surrender and let it flow naturally, until you have settled into a quiet, continuous flow of breathing. And now, in your mind's eye, gently paint a ribbon of breath in the shape of an infinity sign lying on its side and follow the breath as it moves effortlessly throughout the closed loop of the infinity sign. Close your eyes. Silence is key. Create the quietest process you know how. Do this for just a few minutes, and you will feel your body and mind slow down to a place of calm.

At a certain point, you will feel infinity flowing through you. Surrender to it. You have now awakened the Sacred Power of Trust. Feel free to practice Infinity Breath whenever you feel your trust in the moment slipping away. It will always bring you back home.

When we are trusting, we can make choices from an abundance mentality rather than a poverty consciousness. Desperation drifts away, and we can direct our thoughts to the land of infinite possibilities instead of to the place of limiting beliefs. This expanded mind-set helps us make more consciously aligned choices, creating a higher probability that our dreams and desires will come to fruition. And this is where the *Sacred Power of Abundance* takes over.

CHAPTER TWENTY

THE SACRED POWER
OF ABUNDANCE

If your daily life seems poor, do not blame it;
blame yourself, tell yourself that you are not poet
enough to call forth its riches; for the Creator,
there is no poverty.

— Rainer Maria Rilke

When it comes down to conscious decision-making, whatever we end up choosing will become the seed for the next moment, hour, rest of our day, and ultimately the rest of our lives. The process of making a choice is one we were given by our earliest teachers, care-givers, and authority figures. We were taught a particular mind-set in terms of how we should go about choosing things in life. We were trained and punished or rewarded based on the style, process, and methodology we employed and the results we experienced. But, most important, we were conditioned regarding the consequences of our choices. For example, as a child, if you were shown three options and told simply *to choose*, most likely you chose one of the options. You may have thought about choosing more than one or even inquiring about other options, but that was frowned upon. So whenever that moment first happened, you shrunk your world-view on what was available to you. Most of our problem solving in school laid out a few options and instructed us to choose only one. We were encouraged to answer solely based on what was provided. Coloring outside the lines, or choosing outside of the options provided, was considered "not following directions." Most times, if we were told to pick from three options, we were rarely, if ever, celebrated for coming up with a creative solution or a fourth option.

The *Sacred Power of Abundance* shatters all the constrictions that seemed logical in school. This power encourages us in every moment to think infinitely, reach beyond, and explore new, novel, untried options. Abundance is a mind-set and an orientation to existence that offers infinite choices in every moment. Inherently, we know this to be true, which is why we continuously quest after new solutions to problems that have existed for centuries.

THE PIE IS BIG AND GETTING BIGGER

When we look to our most genuine selves—beneath our flesh casing, beyond life's drama, and outside of the moment-to-moment conditioning we have bought into or self-imposed—we see that life's richness is available to us in every moment. We are open to a vast infinity of wealth consciousness. Even when it so obviously appears that there is only one ticket left, only one option available, or a single slice of the pie remaining, these are simply illusions of the moment. In reality, the pie is big . . . really big, and growing bigger.

The *Sacred Power of Abundance* always guides us *to place our attention on meeting our needs* rather than the constriction or blockage that separates us from the fulfillment of that need. But a mind-set conditioned with poverty consciousness tends to focus on perceived limitations. That gap between what we desire in a given moment and what appears to be available can be a powerful spark for our creative solution. Awakening the *Sacred Power of Abundance* reveals that the pie is ever expanding, and there is more of everything if we shatter the way we see the world. When we look really deep, we realize that the fear, lack, and poverty consciousness we often embrace are indeed self-imposed or projected on us by what we read, hear, and see. But that's not who we are. The *Divine Principle of Infinite Flow* has taught us that we are open conduits for the magnificent flow of the abundant cosmos. We are divinely designed to experience the most expanded, unconstricted, ever-evolving, and Universal aspects of our Self that are pregnant with possibilities.

The *Sacred Power of Abundance* dovetails seamlessly with the *Sacred Power of Trust*. Whether we call it wealth consciousness, abundance consciousness, infinity consciousness, or unbounded awareness, when we are in that state—embracing all the Universe has to offer—we place no conditions on what we are prepared to receive. We are fully open. These are the powerful moments where we say "Yes!" to every offer and where happiness seems to chase us.

The *Sacred Power of Abundance* invites us to open our arms so wide that *everything*—money, health, love, forgiveness, opportunity, happiness, spirit—flows into us without conditions.

WHERE DOES MONEY FIT IN?

Having lots of money doesn't always provide happiness. It definitely provides the opportunity to not have to *worry* about money but not necessarily anything else. And you can still have lots of money and worry that it's not enough or that you'll lose it. The world is filled with unhappy people who have lots of money and happy people who have no money. It's also filled with miserable people lacking in material possessions and ecstatic people with really large bank accounts. But without an abundance mind-set regarding the other aspects of life, happiness will most likely elude you . . . even if you're sitting on a big pile of cash.

Just as trust is built on the foundation of infinite flow, abundance consciousness is a perspective in which we see *all of life* as an infinite interdependent, interwoven fabric that connects every aspect of existence and *flows* through us in every moment. Every breath we take creates a vacuum of air that will be filled by another person's exhale. Every word we speak enters the silence, alters it, vibrates, and creates the potential for a word from someone else. Every conversation we have is not simply the beginning of something but a continuation of everything that has led up to that moment. Where will the money you need come from? Wherever it is right now!

EVERY MOMENT IS A CO-CREATION

Since the *Sacred Power of Abundance* is built on the *Divine Principle of Infinite Flow*, there must be continuous circulation. To thrive and experience the abundance of life, we must keep it going. If we flow our generosity out into the world, but don't allow ourselves to receive the same kindness from others, we exhaust our supply and ultimately we collapse. And if we are focused on hoarding our abundance—only receiving—and not sharing it with others, we become energetically constipated.

The two-way exchange flows infinitely and if we open ourselves to it, we become it. We are the evolutionary co-creator of every sunrise and every sunset, every birth and every death, every laugh and every tear, every bark and every meow, and every seed and every falling leaf, combined with all the matter and all the energy of the world that has ever existed. That's a lot of co-creation!

When we allow the world to lovingly flow into us with open arms and then let it flow out of us with grace and generosity, we become a conduit for whatever we desire. And it is in that sweet act of simultaneously nourishing *and* receiving nourishment that we fulfill our purpose, our needs, our desires, and the Universe's intentions.

LIVING ABUNDANCE

Right now, to embrace this sacred power, let's commit to flowing *and* accepting the love, the forgiveness, the compassion, the generosity, the money, the compliments, the support, the health, the nourishment, the peace, and the abundance of life in all its forms as it weaves through the five realms of our existence—the physical, emotional, material, relationship, and spiritual aspects of each moment. We are all connected. We are all stardust. We are all one. Let's stay open to abundance consciousness; and always remember that you are not just *in the Universe* but that *the whole Universe is resting inside of you*. To spark the *Sacred Power of Abundance* in your life, pick a day of the week and just say "Yes!" to every opportunity that comes to you. Don't let fear, laziness, a feeling of being overwhelmed, or constriction stand in your way. Just say yes and see what happens. You will be inviting the abundance of the Universe to begin rushing its riches into your life.

CHAPTER TWENTY-ONE

THE SACRED POWER OF SHAKTI

The Universe has shouted itself alive.
We are one of the shouts.

— Ray Bradbury

Once awakened, the *Sacred Powers of Trust and Abundance* effortlessly align you with the infinite flow of the Universe and expand your ability to receive its magnificence. But it is through the *Sacred Power of Shakti* that you activate a transformational shift in every aspect of your life, converting that Infinite Flow into a very personal expression of the dreams and desires of the Universe.

THE MOST POWERFUL ENERGY

In the ancient wisdom teachings, the highest vibration of Spirit that flows through all existence is called *Shakti*. Considered the Life Force of the Universe, Shakti is believed to be the most powerful expression of Divine Feminine Energy. Shakti is pure, ecstatic, creative, authentic, nourishing, healing, restorative, life-affirming, and transformational. Shakti holds a sacred space in ancient devotional rituals and modern spiritual practices and is worshipped with deep reverence and often depicted as a woman, a goddess, a mother, a warrior, a priestess, a healer, and as God, expressed as the Divine Mother.

165

Shakti is the most powerful energy in the Universe and vibrates at the highest frequency because it is five-dimensional. Not only does this Sacred Power run through our world in the *three dimensions* of physical form. It also flows through our being as a pure, invisible, energetic life force in the *fourth dimension*, rippling through our energy body, also known as our subtle or astral body. But, most important, Shakti has a fifth-dimensional quality—*the ability to merge* our physical existence with the invisible, nonlocal, formless world *in order to manifest our intentions into tangible reality!*

A TRANSFORMATIONAL FUSION BEYOND TIME AND SPACE

This fifth-dimensional cosmic merging of Shakti energy is the game changer of all existence. The *Sacred Power of Shakti* inherently carries with it the ability to turn intangible thoughts, wishes, dreams, and desires into tangible outcomes. Harnessing the *Sacred Power of Shakti* awakens your capacity to transform mind into matter. Shakti goes beyond simply letting us peek into other realms. *It is the true cosmic merging of all realms that co-exist in the Universe*—the physical (tangible) realm, the subtle (psychological) realm, and the causal (spiritual) realm. When the *Sacred Power of Shakti* is rippling through you, it allows you to simultaneously have one foot in the physical realm and one foot in the vast expanse of the infinite.

Shakti is that potent spark that transforms thoughts into things—it's the actionable process of manifestation. Einstein referred to the power of Shakti as "spooky action at a distance." Even he couldn't quite understand it because it is so mindblowing. Right now Shakti energy is rippling through your body like an electric current *simultaneously* connecting you to the past, present, and future. It's rippling through every moment that has ever existed *and* every moment *that will ever exist!* Shakti energy is timeless, boundless, within you, beyond you, tangible, and intangible, filled with activity and stillness—*all at the same time.*

AWAKENING THE SACRED POWER OF SHAKTI

And yet, on a very personal level, we can effortlessly awaken our *Sacred Power of Shakti* and channel the cosmic flow directly into and through our very being. Yes! You and I can harness the divine energy of the Universe. And as long as we are willing to trust and let abundance flow through us, the *Sacred Power of Shakti* is available to us in every moment.

THE SACRED ENERGETIC CONNECTIONS WITHIN YOUR BODY

In the ancient wisdom traditions, the *Sacred Powers of Transformation* were located in seven distinct energy centers located in the physical body. Ancient India referred to these energy centers as *chakras* (translated as "turnings" or "wheels"), and it was believed that these seven wheels of energy were the junction points between our physical, mental, and spiritual worlds, such that all the energy of the Universe converged at seven vortexes within the human body. Modern acupuncture and acupressure practitioners use these meridians as healing points, and according to the ancient wisdom traditions of the Sufis in Persia, the Hindus in India, and the Hopi Indians of North America, these energetic convergences were domains of transformation and manifestation.

DIVINE CONVERGENCE

The 5,000-year-old Indian healing system known as Ayurveda teaches that these seven core energy centers are gateways connecting us to the physical world we live in and to the unknown world beyond us—powerful focal points for the reception and transmission of Shakti energy.

These seven junction points also house our relationships, our creativity, our dreams and desires, our ability to receive and give love, our voice, our choices, our purpose, our connection to self, and our connection to source. And within our physical body, these seven sacred spaces are also the largest concentration of our blood vessels, nerve endings, hormonal surges, electrical wiring, immune functions, digestion of food, experiences, and emotions, and the vital energy that fuels our breathing, tickles our brain, and beats our heart.

The Seven Chakras—Their Meanings and Vibrations

spirit —— om

insight —— shaam

voice —— haam

love —— yaam

power —— raam

creativity —— vaam

connection —— laam

The divine convergence that occurs in each of these seven access points has the power to effortlessly balance, heal, and transform you in every aspect of your life—manifesting your simple desires and fulfilling your most ambitious dreams. The capacity of these personal vortexes is limited only by your own beliefs.

CHANNELING SHAKTI

The seven main chakras are aligned in a column that begins at the base of your spine and extends to the top of your head. They're located symmetrically up your body, each spaced a distance of approximately seven fingers from each other, which is one hand width and two additional fingers from the tailbone to a bit below the navel, to the center of your torso behind your abdomen (called the solar plexus), to your heart, to your throat, to the third eye (an inch or so above your eyebrows), and then to the crown of your head.

The oldest wisdom traditions from Asia, India, the Middle East, and North and South America integrated the *Sacred Power of Shakti* into their cultures thousands of years ago. Devotional ceremonies in ancient China, Egypt, Tibet, Turkey, and Persia all celebrated their spiritual leaders' ability to awaken Shakti and harness its energy to control the forces of nature, and awaken supernatural powers. You have that exact same ability to awaken Shakti and harness its energy through your chakras. And once you are comfortable with the process, you will begin to manifest your own dreams and desires.

WIDENING THE LANES ON YOUR SHAKTI SUPERHIGHWAY

Each chakra has a specific color associated with it that grows brighter as the energy center is awakened and opened. When the light is at its brightest, this means there are no blockages or obstructions and that you have opened your energy center as widely as possible (similar to opening up additional toll lanes on a highway, so the traffic can flow more easily and quickly). Once all seven chakras are opened wide, the *Sacred Power of Shakti* flows into you, through you, and out of you easily and smoothly. Once Shakti energy is rushing through you without obstruction, everything inside of you aligns and begins to merge with everything outside of you. That means that every seed you plant on the inside blossoms and blooms on the outside, leading to a natural and effortless manifestation.

YOUR AWARENESS CARRIES DIVINE ENERGY

Earlier, when we explored the *Second Divine Principle of Awareness*, we learned that your awareness carries sacred energy. And we connected to the *Sacred Powers of Attention* and *Intention* as a starting point for our journey of personal transformation. Additionally, these two *Sacred Powers* are considered the key to the process of *Shakti Manifestation*—an ancient energetic healing technique once reserved exclusively for spiritual masters and advanced practitioners. Here's how it works: By placing our *attention* on a specific chakra and then planting an *intention* in its fertile soil, we activate the flow of Shakti in that sacred space. When we do this to all seven of our chakras, we have essentially carved out a new riverbed for divine energy to flow through us. This can be quite jarring to the uninitiated, because you are instantly aligned with a boundless flow of Shakti energy. It's essentially the difference between sipping water slowly through a straw or having a rushing waterfall cascading down on you.

This ancient practice of awakening each of the seven energy centers and inviting Shakti Manifestation to flow through them was often cautioned against because of the speed of the energy current and the potential for spontaneous manifestation with massive life-changing impact. It's not for everyone. But that's the reason you and I are here right now . . . bold, powerful, evolutionary, personal transformation. So as long as you proceed calmly, gently, and with divine purpose, you will experience the life-affirming shift you are looking for without any negative side effects.

SHAKTI MANIFESTATION

When we practice Shakti Manifestation, we invite divine energy into our body through our root chakra . . . our lowest and heaviest energy center . . . where we are most connected to the earth. We then invite this flow to move farther upward, and enter each of the energetic conversion touch points. As Shakti rises, and arrives at the edges of each energy center, it coaxes that chakra to match its vibration in a process called *attunement*. This chakra tuning process heightens the frequency of the energy center—activating the purpose of that chakra—and causing the colored light within it to glow more brightly and radiate outward in every direction.

Flowing ever higher, the flow of Shakti ultimately arrives at the seventh energy center—the crown chakra—our lightest, most subtle chakra. And once that junction point is awakened, the circuit is complete with pure, unbounded, infinite energy flowing into your root, rippling upward through all of your chakras, and activating your intentions and their divine connection to the infinite. Shakti then flows back out of your crown, reuniting you with the eternal vibration where your essence is merged with pure, divine cosmic flow.

Shakti Manifestation is one of the most powerful of the sacred practices. And from this fully aligned and awakened state, your intentions and desires are whispered into the unmanifest world, where everything is possible. Shakti stretches the finite into the infinite . . . expands the time-bound into the timeless . . . and erases the earthbound limitations of practical reality, societal constraints, and emotional constrictions.

So let's do it!

CHAPTER TWENTY-TWO

SHAKTI MANIFESTATION

*Within all of us is a divine process to manifest
and attract all that we need and desire.*

— Dr. Wayne Dyer

We can practice Shakti Manifestation right now as we explore each of the seven chakras and awaken the connection between our personal expression and the divine Universal expression that rests at our core.

THE FIRST CHAKRA—CONNECTION

The first chakra, also called the root or base chakra, is known in Sanskrit as the *Muladhara* (pronounced moola-dara). This is your most primal energy center, which establishes your basic needs of safety, security, and connection—connection to the earth, the world around you, your physical body . . . your family . . . your tribe . . . and your community. This chakra establishes your groundedness and stability as you flow through life, and therefore it is the heaviest of chakras. When Shakti energy is flowing freely through the root, we feel good in our skin, secure and confident that we can easily fulfill our needs; our connections are balanced; we come from a place of centeredness and sturdiness. When this chakra is constricted or its energy is blocked, we can feel anxious, unsafe, and worried, coming from a place of fear and instability. We feel disconnected from our relationships, separated from a true sense of community. Are you feeling connected right now or distant from the world around you? Are you feeling centered in yourself?

The root chakra is located at the tip of the tailbone and is essentially your contact point to the earth when you sit on the floor or ground. This is the site of your physical connection to the world. Traditionally, the Muladhara is associated with the color red. During a Shakti Manifestation, this root is where the foundational flow of all the Universe's energy enters you. So the flow of anything from the unmanifest, the unseen, the unbirthed, or the infinite enters here. The ancient vibration or seed mantra for the first chakra is *Laam*. Let's awaken that aspect of our being and let Shakti flow in by envisioning a red ball of light at the tip of our tailbone, placing our fingers on that space, taking a long, slow, deep breath in, and chanting the vibration LAAM long and loud as we exhale. Do it now. Can you feel your root opening to let Shakti in?

THE SECOND CHAKRA—CREATIVITY

The second chakra, also called the sacral or sex chakra, is known in Sanskrit as the *Svadhisthana* (pronounced svah-dee-shtana) chakra. This is your creativity center where all new expressions of your existence are birthed and REbirthed. The second chakra is where you plant all the seeds of new beginnings, ideas, projects, ways of seeing the world, behaviors, relationships, directions, and beliefs. This is where the unconditioned aspect of your being awakens; where you take your very first steps into uncharted territory—the unknown, the rich, the fresh, the uncertain. How's your creativity?

The most powerful energy on the planet is creative energy. And it is the energy of birthing that transforms thought into action, concept into product, idea into utterance, desire into fulfillment, and intention into manifestation. The second chakra is located a few inches below your navel and is traditionally associated with the color orange.

When Shakti energy is flowing freely through the second chakra, you are full of possibilities and move in the direction of your dreams; your creative juices flow in all areas of your life; you imagine, invent, design, envision, and nurture; your beauty, sexuality, and sensuality are enlivened; you flow effortlessly into renewal, REbirth, and rejuvenation. Your creative expression is energized, and you are not afraid to dream big. However, when this chakra is constricted or energy is blocked in any way, we cling to the comfort of the familiar—we hold fast to routine—even when it no longer serves us. We resist dreaming big for fear of failing. We play small. We suppress our emotions. And we can feel stuck, limited, holding on to beliefs, paths, ideas, people, jobs, habits, attitudes, or sentiments that stand in our way or hold us back.

During a Shakti Manifestation, this chakra is where the divine, creative energy of the Universe is sparked inside of you. The ancient vibration or seed mantra for the second chakra is *Vaam*.

Let's awaken that aspect of our being and let Shakti flow in by envisioning an orange ball of light a few inches below our belly button, placing our fingers on that space, taking a long, slow, deep breath in, and chanting the vibration VAAM loud and long as we exhale. Do it now. Do you feel this chakra opening?

THE THIRD CHAKRA—POWER

The third chakra, also called the solar plexus chakra, is known in Sanskrit as the *Manipura* (pronounced monny-poora). Often referred to as the *Power Center*, this chakra moves you forward and helps you follow through in the direction of the seeds you've planted in the fertile ground of your second chakra. The manipura is located in the center of your chest at your solar plexus, a few inches below the joining of your rib cage. This is essentially the center of your body, where your emotional and physical digestive fires burn most brightly. This radiating power plant moves you toward your target and awakens your personal, internal strength to achieve your intentions and desires. This is the "lock it down," "get it done" *manifestation* energy center. Traditionally associated with the color yellow, this chakra radiates like the sun from our solar plexus—evolving, metabolizing, and transforming us in every moment. Are you feeling your power?

When Shakti energy is flowing freely through the solar plexus, we are empowered to follow through on the creative projects and visions we first sparked in the second chakra. This energy center is often referred to as the "excuse" chakra because, when this chakra is constricted or energy is blocked in any way, we procrastinate, hold off, and make excuses. The ancient vibration or seed mantra for the third chakra is *Raam*.

Let's awaken that aspect of our being, move past our excuses, and let Shakti flow in by envisioning a yellow ball of light in the center of our solar plexus, placing our fingers on that space, taking a long, slow, deep breath in, and chanting the vibration RAAM loud and long as we exhale. Do it now. Do you feel your power center opening?

THE FOURTH CHAKRA—THE HEART

The fourth chakra, also called the heart chakra, is known in Sanskrit as the *Anahata* (pronounced anna-hatta) chakra. This is your personal connection to love, kindness, compassion, empathy, forgiveness, and peace. The Anahata is located near your physical heart, in the center of your chest. You can place your hands on your heart right now and breathe in and feel the love flowing in and out of you. Traditionally, it is associated with the color green.

As Shakti energy flows into the heart chakra, it awakens the physical properties of our heart *and* the nonphysical, more Universal, heart-based expressions of love. Timeless wisdom teaches that the *source of all kindness is self-kindness*; the source of all compassion is *self-compassion*; the source of all forgiveness is *self-forgiveness*; and the source of all love is *self-love*. As the fourth chakra is awakened by this powerful and sacred energy, your deep desires of the heart begin to expand and merge with the physical, emotional, energetic, and spiritual aspects of your existence. How open is your heart?

When Shakti energy is flowing freely through our fifth chakra, a magnificent expression of the *Divine Principle of Infinite Flow* unfolds. The finite merges with the infinite as the heart-based seeds of intention you've planted in the fertile soil of your heart begin their journey of manifestation. Barriers to receiving love start to melt as you become more accepting, more forgiving, more understanding, and more compassionate. Once this expression of *pure love manifestation* takes hold, you become more attractive to love. Sweet, tender, divine affection begins to visit you, then follow you, then chase you, until it ripples through you. And in return, gratitude radiates back out into the world.

When this chakra is constricted or energy is blocked in any way, it is a sign that we have stopped trusting—essentially, that we have suspended our belief in the *Divine Principle of Infinite Flow*. We feel separate from the boundless current of Universal love. This is where we get confused—thinking that love is "out there" somewhere instead of surrendering to it and allowing it to bathe us in unconditional loving-kindness. When there is congestion in this energy center, we hold onto grievances; we resist forgiving; we don't trust our heart; we are skeptical of others' kindness; in essence, we forget that we are so worthy of receiving love and happiness in every moment. The ancient vibration or seed mantra for the heart chakra is *Yum* also pronounced *Yaam*. Let's awaken that aspect of our being and let Shakti flow in by envisioning a green ball of light in the center of our heart, placing our fingers on that space, taking a long, slow, deep breath in, and chanting the vibration YUM long and loud as we exhale. Do it now. Do you feel your heart opening?

THE FIFTH CHAKRA—EXPRESSION

The fifth energy center, the throat chakra, is known in Sanskrit as the *Vishuddha* (pronounced vi-*shoo*-da) chakra. This is your expression center—the house of your voice. The actual vibration that starts in your belly, moves up your chest, enters your throat, arrives at your mouth, and leaves your lips to become your voice in the world, where you express your personal self and your most

Universal Self. Our throat chakra is located at the center of your neck in the middle of your throat, and is traditionally associated with the color blue. How open is your throat chakra?

The throat chakra is our sacred space of multidimensional expression—the words we speak, emotions we convey, body language we exhibit, attitudes we share, the aura we radiate. And it goes deeper than that: your "voice" is also the best expression of who you believe you are—your "truth," your "purpose," your reason for being, your "higher Self." This is essentially the best version of who you can be, where God, Jesus, the Divine Mother, or the Universe speaks through you.

It is from this fifth chakra that you give yourself permission to truly express your native energies as you move throughout the world.

When Shakti energy is flowing freely through the throat chakra, it means you have given yourself permission to fully accept all aspects of yourself—embrace all your light and your darkness, your magnificence and your imperfections, your strengths and your weaknesses—to truly step into your power, allow the Universe to work through you, fully own your impact, and finally let your voice be heard!

When this chakra is constricted or energy is blocked, it is often a sign that you are repressing some aspect of yourself—dimming your light, holding back, biting your tongue, walking on eggshells, or withholding permission to fully flow your most authentic self.

The ancient vibration or seed mantra for the fifth chakra is *Haam*. Let's awaken that aspect of our being and let Shakti flow in by envisioning a blue ball of light at the center of our throat, placing our fingers on that space, taking a long, slow, deep breath in, and chanting the vibration HAAM loud and long as we exhale. Let's do it now. Do you notice the true power of your voice is expanding?

THE SIXTH CHAKRA—INSIGHT

The sixth chakra, also called the third-eye chakra, is known in Sanskrit as the *Ajna* (pronounced *ahjj*-na) chakra, and it's traditionally associated with the color purple. This energy center is where your insight and intuition rests—and it's located in the middle of your lower forehead, between your eyes and up a bit. Throughout history, there has been a distinct relationship between the third eye and mystical or spiritual properties. How open is your third eye?

When Shakti energy is flowing freely through our third eye, we make more conscious choices . . . our decisions become more purposeful, coming from a place of clarity rather than from fear or desperation. As this chakra awakens, we truly begin to *see*, and our judgment heightens. The bigger picture guides our perceptions and our selections. When this chakra is constricted or energy is blocked in any way, we make conditioned, knee-jerk decisions out of fear or desperation; we question our choice-making; and we stop trusting that the Universe will deliver us to exactly where we need to be.

The ancient vibration or seed mantra for the sixth chakra is *Shaam.* Let's awaken that aspect of our being and let Shakti awaken our conscious choice-maker by envisioning a blue ball of light at the center of our third eye, placing our fingers on that space, taking a long, slow, deep breath in, and chanting the vibration SHAAM long and loud as we exhale. Do it now. Can you feel your third eye opening?

THE SEVENTH CHAKRA—SOURCE

The seventh chakra, or crown chakra, is known in Sanskrit as the *Sahaswara* (pronounced sah-ha-*swa*-rah) translated as "the thousand-petaled-lotus" chakra. Located at the crown of your head, this is where the Shakti energy that has just awakened your six lower chakras rises one more time, activates the intentions of the seventh chakra, and pours out into the ether to complete the circuit. The crown chakra is considered the lightest energy center and has the power to divinely connect you to Source. Traditionally, this energy center is associated with the color white or ultraviolet—essentially, beyond the spectrum of all colors.

As your seventh chakra opens, every intention you have planted in each chakra regarding your relationships, dreams, creativity, power, heart, voice, and connection to Source are merged with the unbounded, infinite, expanding flow of the universe. This is the Sacred Power of Shakti demonstrating the *Divine Principle of Infinite Flow*. When this chakra is constricted or energy is blocked in any way, we can feel anxious, unsafe, and worried, coming from a place of fear and instability. We feel separate from the wholeness of the Divine.

When Shakti energy is flowing freely through the seventh chakra, everything that has just flowed through you flows back out into the Universe. The light in each chakra grows from a pinpoint to a giant glowing orb that extends way beyond your physical body. Opening up the crown chakra transcends your limiting beliefs, providing you full access to the entire universe of possibilities. This is you in your most Universal state, purely merging your sense of self—your individuality and ego—with the divine one-ness of existence. The ancient vibration or seed mantra for the seventh chakra is *Om*. Let's awaken that aspect of our being and let Shakti flow through us by envisioning an ultraviolet ball of light at the crown of our head, placing our fingers on that space, taking a long, slow, deep breath in, and chanting the vibration OM long and loud as we exhale. Do it now.

MANIFESTING

We've done it! We've opened all our chakras and begun the flow of sweet Shakti. With every breath, we align our essence with the infinite flow of the Universe. Once you have opened all seven chakras by chanting their vibrations, simply surrender to the flow of Shakti energy entering you through the root chakra and grounding you, sparking your creativity, strengthening your power, expanding your heart, heightening your expression, clarifying your insight, and flowing you back into Source. This is pure Shakti Manifestation. Let's take it deeper through some daily practices.

CHAPTER TWENTY-THREE

LIVING WITH INFINITE FLOW

Each day provides its own gifts.

— Marcus Aurelius

THE DAILY PRACTICES

You can awaken the *Divine Principle of Infinite Flow* in your life and the *Sacred Powers of Trust, Abundance,* and *Shakti* through five powerful daily practices that can be used individually or in combination. Each practice offers you an opportunity to cultivate trust, abundance, and Shakti energy. All five practiced on a daily basis will nourish your own infinite flow and merge you with pure consciousness. The five daily rituals are:

1. Asking the Four Sacred Questions of *Infinite Flow*
2. The *Shakti Manifestation* Meditation
3. The Sacred Affirmation of Infinite Flow
4. Performing the Sacred Rite of Infinite Flow
5. The Daily Mantra of Infinite Flow

Asking the Four Sacred Questions
for the Divine Principle of Infinite Flow

When we first sit down for our morning ritual, we begin by asking ourselves Four Sacred Questions. These are Infinite Flow questions designed to remind us of our eternal stardust relationship with the Universe—the trust we can have in every moment, the abundance that is our birthright, and the Shakti energy that flows through our physical body, our astral body, the entire Universe, and our Soul. We close our eyes, place our hands over our hearts, and silently ask each question for a minute. Sometimes answers will flow. Sometimes there will be no answers. When you have completed the process, take a long, slow, deep breath in and release all the questions and any answers that arose. It's very common for answers to come back to you hours or days later. The key is to ask the Sacred Questions over and over until they become part of your inner dialogue. In time they will also become part of your outer dialogue, as you begin to trust unconditionally, and see *your* world as an expression of abundant, infinite, ever-expanding Shakti.

And this is how energy effortlessly transforms from questions to answers to awakenings to choices to actions to transformation.

The Four Sacred Questions to Awaken Infinite Flow in Your Life

We ask *Four Sacred Questions* to expand our ability to trust, acknowledge our ever-flowing abundance, and activate the power of Shakti energy in our life.

1. *Where do I see the Universe in me?*

2. *Where in my life can I trust more?*

3. *What are the ways I can open myself to the abundance of the Universe?*

4. *How can I surrender right now to the Sacred Power of Shakti?*

By asking the Sacred Questions, we begin an internal conversation that starts to translate our thoughts, dreams, and desires into the tangible reality of our outer world. We accelerate the materializing of brainwaves into inspirations—and intentions into actions—by infusing the transformation process with Shakti energy.

The Infinite Flow Meditation—Shakti Manifestation

For thousands of years, spiritual leaders have used the power of Shakti to awaken, nourish, heal, and transform. Through Shakti Manifestation rituals, they've turned darkness into light, poverty into abundance, emptiness into wholeness, weakness into strength, sickness into health, and disbelief into faith. There are two ways to proceed here:

1. Simply practice the Shakti Manifestation from the previous chapter.

2. Visit davidji.com/SacredBonus, where I will walk you through an expanded Shakti audio guided meditation called *The Infinite Flow Meditation*, which will awaken, attune, and harmonize all seven of your chakras, aligning you with the flow of the Universe and merging your intentions with the intentions of the Divine. Feel free to visit now and see what it feels like to close your eyes and be guided through a powerful chakra awakening.

Remember, you can perform Shakti Manifestation anytime by closing your eyes, putting your attention on each chakra, and bringing an intention to it. This can be in the form of chanting, speaking, whispering, or silently repeating an affirmation (*I am creative, I am worthy of love, I am whole,* and so on) or the sounds of each chakra (Laam, Vaam, Raam, Yaam, Haam, Shaam, Om). Just the simple act of combining single-pointed attention on your chakras and the subtle intention to open and receive will bring an expansion into your energetic body.

The Sacred Affirmation of Infinite Flow

There is a Sacred Affirmation that has been uttered for thousands of years to awaken trust, abundance, and Shakti energy. Rumored to be based on 3,000-year-old folklore, the tale begins with King Solomon asking his chief adviser to bring him a ring that could make him happy when he was sad. The 12th-century Persian Sufi poet Attar of Nishapur chronicled a similar scenario when he cited an ancient Eastern monarch in need of some "miraculous" item that would lift his queen's depression. The legend explains that in both cases, an oracle was summoned, secretly told about the predicament, and then dispatched on a mission to solve this eternal dilemma. The stories parallel a similar narrative with both sages traveling far and wide, seeking insights from sorcerers, wizards, holy men, and magicians. In the end, they both found a "mystical jeweler" who crafted a solution by forging a ring inscribed with the words, "This too shall pass," which in Solomon's case was the Hebrew "gam zeh ya'avor."

King Solomon was purported to have been very pleased with the result as the ring instantly turned his sadness to a state of happiness. But with bittersweet brilliance, it also reminded him of the impermanence of life and that this new state of non-sadness would also pass. These teachings are rooted in the *Divine Principle of Infinite Flow*, which always reminds us to trust in the Universe.

We can awaken *Infinite Flow* in our lives by starting the day with this *Sacred Affirmation*:

Every day, in every way, I flow
the divine blessings of the Universe.

And throughout the day, we repeat, "Every day, in every way, I flow the divine blessings of the Universe" whenever we sense we are feeling separate from the divine flow of the Universe or thinking with a poverty consciousness. We may have felt this way in the past; but from this moment forward, there is no need. The truth is that the infinite Universe rests within you and *you* are the perfect expression of the *Divine Principle of Infinite Flow*.

By ritualizing the *Sacred Affirmation*, you reinvite your participation in the infinite flow of the Universe and awaken your ability to trust, flow abundance, and harness the *Sacred Power of Shakti* energy. I also like to use the Hebrew mantra: *gam zeh ya'avor* in moments of acute physical or emotional pain. It short-circuits my sadness or discomfort and reminds me that help is on the way!

Performing the Sacred Rite of Infinite Flow

We've asked the Sacred Questions, awakened the flow of Shakti energy through a chakra meditation, and silently repeated the Sacred Affirmation. Now it's time to connect your physical body with your heart and mind with a Sacred Rite.

Stand up, feet shoulder width apart. Start off by placing your palms together and bringing them to your heart in a prayer position. Now extend your arms as widely to the side as you can reach, opening your chest as widely as possible. Drift your attention to the tip of your tailbone. See it in your mind's eye, feel it, and with your eyes closed, feel a powerful surge of healing expansive energy enter your body through the tip of your tailbone. Take a long, slow deep breath in and envision the Universe rushing upward through your body, flowing through each chakra, and pouring out through the top of your head as you exhale loudly, "Shakti!" Practice this five times right now, and see how it feels.

The Daily Mantra of Infinite Flow

Next we add a mantra to follow us throughout the day to awaken your *Sacred Powers of Trust, Abundance*, and *Shakti*:

I FLOW. I FLOW. I FLOW.

As situations unfold around you that challenge, disappoint, or constrict your energetic flow, awaken your ability to effortlessly flow by saying out loud, whispering, or repeating silently:

I FLOW (as you inhale). I FLOW (as you exhale).
I FLOW (as you inhale).

When it comes to the *Divine Principle of Infinite Flow*, remember:

1. Trust is believing that the Universe that has powered you through every challenging moment of your life will deliver you to exactly where you need to be.

2. The Universe is abundant—only constricted thinking makes you play small.

3. In any moment you can awaken the Shakti energy that is resting inside and align yourself with the cosmic flow.

So far, we've journeyed on four Divine Paths, discovered four powerful Secrets, embedded four Divine Principles, and awakened their Sacred Powers. Gently allow all this timeless wisdom to integrate into your Soul. When you are ready, we'll take our steps onto the Fifth Divine Path.

The Fifth Secret

THE DIVINE
PRINCIPLE OF
INNER FIRE

The Divine Principle of Inner Fire
and
the Sacred Powers of
Your Awakened Heart . . . Passion . . .
and Purpose

CHAPTER TWENTY-FOUR

WALKING THE FIFTH DIVINE PATH

The Fire of Transformation

Faeries, come take me out of this dull world,
For I would ride with you upon the wind,
Run on top of the disheveled tide,
And dance upon the mountains like a flame.

— William Butler Yeats

THE CATALYST OF LIFE

The eternal flame that first ignited the entire Universe burns inside of you as well. You are not just created from stardust; you also share that same divine fire that lights every star in the galaxy and that flows through every atom on this planet and cell in your body.

This inner fire is the source of your passion, your clarity, your creativity, your courage, your compassion, your forgiveness, your purpose, your love, and your sense of personal power. It is the catalyst of life that ignites our will to act and transform the raw materials of our intentions, dreams, and desires into tangible form. And yet so often this flame is sleeping silently inside us, waiting for a spark of inspiration to light it. When our inner fire is dormant or in a weakened state, our passion is sedated, our energy is low, and we lack the inspiration to do what is needed to manifest our intentions. But this fire can also rage, spewing red-hot embers and rivers of molten lava, blistering everything in its path as it scorches the village and everyone in it.

The Divine Principle of Inner Fire is based on the ancient formula for the origin of all existence. These teachings are the foundation for the 5,000-year-old Indian healing system of Ayurveda, which I have studied and practiced for more than a decade. Whatever your belief system is regarding the creation of the Universe, here's my translation of how Ayurveda says it all started:

> In the beginning, there was just space . . . cold emptiness . . . the void . . . the vast expanse of nothingness. But what does space do? Nothing. It just sits there . . . totally still . . . holding space . . . and holding space . . . and holding space for trillions of years. But ultimately space wanted to experience itself, so it began folding itself back in on itself to feel itself . . . see itself . . . witness itself. In the ancient Indian wisdom traditions, this process of the Self curving in back on itself in order to experience itself is called *namaha*. And as space began to curve back in on itself, air was created out of the movement. And as more air was generated with each movement of namaha, friction was created. And as the air moved more quickly, and the frequency of friction accelerated, sparks began to fly and then a flicker of a flame . . . and then fire began to rage through the heavens. And as this uncontrollable fire licked the edges of the Universe, the heat met the icy cold of the galaxy and condensation was formed. And in time, billions of drops of water began to slowly drip down the edges of the cosmos, solidifying, taking shape, and ultimately creating the element of earth. Five master elements at the very core of reality: *Space. Air. Fire. Water. Earth.*

Twelve billion years later, these are the same five master elements that make up every single aspect of your existence—the seen and the unseen. They are the most Universal expressions of life and your most personal ones as well. The original flame that started it all is nourished inside of you with each breath of Shakti energy you take. And it is the *Divine Principle of Inner Fire* that determines how you ignite your very next moment—awakening your desires; crystalizing your vision; sparking your intentions; burning away unwanted thoughts, beliefs, ideas, and memories; and fueling your next leap in the direction of your dreams.

The journey of life is fraught with many wrong turns, dead ends, and confusing signs along the way. Walking this Fifth Divine Path and uncovering its secret will help you avoid many of the pitfalls and heartaches that can otherwise distract you and send you reeling backwards. Each day can bring a bewildering swirl of love, passion, and purpose as we relentlessly question our emotions, the status of our lifelong desires, and the deeper meaning of each moment. The *Divine Principle of Inner Fire* cuts through the confusion, reawakening and leading you. Navigating the cosmic expanse of our inner fire and mastering its magnificence is a lifelong endeavor requiring heightened intuition, sensitivity, awareness, and commitment. The corresponding Sacred Powers will be your life-affirming guides on your journey of burning brightly:

The Sacred Power of Your Awakened Heart

The Sacred Power of Passion

The Sacred Power of Purpose

CHAPTER TWENTY-FIVE

THE SACRED POWER OF YOUR AWAKENED HEART

The best and most beautiful things in the world cannot be seen or even touched—they must be felt with the heart.

— Helen Keller

THE DRUMBEAT OF THE UNIVERSE

Place your hand on your heart. This is the space where 70 times each minute, the most active muscle in your body receives blue carbon-dioxide-filled blood from your veins and pumps it into your lungs, turning it into red oxygen-rich blood in return and squeezing that sweet nectar throughout your body to spark you with life; 108,000 times each day, 36 million times each year. But this tangible muscular organ is simply a metaphor for something deeper and more profound.

The first sound you ever heard was the beating of your mother's heart. It accompanied you for the first nine months of your life in the darkness of the womb, becoming the soundtrack of your earliest period of development. Like the ticking of a clock, it escorted you through every liquid breath you took in the womb, every twinkling of cellular development, every movement you made, every hormonal surge that came into you, every growth spurt, every moment of sleep, and every vibration that rippled around you and through you. One day, as you entered the world of light and took your first breath through air, that sweet comforting drum beat stopped—and you were on your own. As you read these words, that concept of withdrawing from such comfort and familiarity may sound sad—but it is the journey that every human being has taken and it is in that moment of taking your first breath through air that the *Sacred Power of Your Awakened Heart* was transferred from your mother's heart to yours.

MY HEART SPEAKS MY DEEPEST TRUTH

The tenderest part of you is also the strongest part of you. And although it may feel counterintuitive, *in your vulnerability rests your strength*. It's so paradoxical, it might make your head hurt; it might even make your heart hurt. But deep down in the core of your being, you know it's true. Your heart is your truest essence, and for thousands of years, the wisest masters of cosmic teachings shared that precious message with their most devoted followers. Yet in our modern day-to-day grind of life, it seems that other issues take precedence. The physical health of our bodies, how we look and feel, our career, our social circle, our status, our financial security, and our family are just a few areas of our life that often overshadow conversations of the heart. And yet there is a thread that runs through all these parts of your life woven by the *Sacred Power of Your Awakened Heart.*

THE POWER OF BODHICITTA

The eternal wisdom of *Your Awakened Heart* spans every aspect of existence. In the most ancient Buddhist wisdom traditions, the awakened heart was often referred to as the awakened mind. The spontaneous state of being in which you strive solely for awakening, empathy, and compassion for all beings is referred to

as *bodhcitta,* which literally means "awakened mind." The word
Bodhi (as in Buddha) means awakened and *citta* (pronounced
chitta) means mind. And yet the deeper translation of bodhicitta is
awakened heart—the part of you that is so magnificently God-like
that it has the divine power to:

1. Soften anything it touches

2. Assess everything as perfect and pure

3. Perceive every moment unconditionally

4. Be unwavering in its ability to love

It's a paradox combining both ends of the extreme—*so tender*
that it only knows compassion, *yet so strong* that it transcends every
circumstance unconditionally. These were the core teachings of
the Buddha, of Jesus, and, in more modern times, these were the
teachings of Saint Mother Teresa and Martin Luther King, Jr.

Love has an infinite number of translations because there are
an infinite number of possible combinations of lover and loved.
The myriad heart-based relationships we have with other humans,
ourselves, animals, and the world around us—even belief systems,
ideas, and ways of being or doing—are so vast, they can never be
fully quantified. They are ever changing as our levels of attachment change and the dynamic of the moment shifts.

ATTACHMENT OR LOVE?

Because love is real time, ebbing and flowing with every breath,
heartbeat, and thought, it has always been defined as a living,
breathing thing. Let's take the one Universal relationship we all
have, *the love of your parent*—and this can be your biological parent, your caregiver, or the person who raised you. You love your
parent, and then one day they disappoint or frustrate you, and
the dynamic shifts. You argue and then you make up. Does the
love return to exactly the same place it was? Is it a bit more or a
bit less based on what transpired between the two of you? How
has your sense of gratitude shifted? How has your sense of attachment shifted? Do you love someone more if things are going

well? And less if you've had an argument or disagreement? Do you see how conditional your love is based on your level of attachment in the moment?

Right now in your mind's eye, envision a relationship with someone you love or care about that has emotional turbulence, toxicity, or is just in a bad space. Remind yourself of the last conversation you had with this person. How would you define your emotions regarding this person? Irritated? Angry? Embarrassed? Bitter? Aggravated? Disappointed? Frustrated? Resentful? Annoyed? Sad? Fed up? Vengeful? Disgusted? Anxious?

Most likely, the other person doesn't fully understand the detailed world of emotions you feel. Even that can make you angry. But get really clear on that emotion. Say it out loud, "I feel . . ."

Now imagine a tenderness that pierces through any constriction you could have to loving this person or feeling loved by them. See them as an innocent baby thrown into this world pure and whole, then as a child who tried so hard to figure out the rules, then as an adolescent who tamed their own soul. Now see a lifetime of pain and disappointments that have sculpted them into the being they are right now. Now see them with deep compassion and visualize a love so pure that you love this other person even more than you have ever loved them. Bring yourself to the moment where you loved them the most, where love flowed through every thought you had about them and your heart was overwhelmed with loving them so deeply. As you think of that moment right now, allow the emotion you felt back then—connection, joy, compassion, happiness, devotion, gratitude—to ripple through you. This is the flicker of the bodhicitta, the awakened heart.

Saint Mother Teresa used to wash the dirty feet of orphan lepers—the outcasts of the lowest caste system in India and society's untouchables. And yet she described that daily experience as "having the privilege to wash the feet of God."

We are beings of compassion who seek love and belongingness in every moment, and yet we have learned an entire vocabulary to distance our self from its true source because we know and fear the sting of heartache. We crave attention, affection, appreciation, and acceptance. We search for approval, validation, and acknowledgment. We desire so desperately to be held and loved, cherished and cheered, listened to and heard. We have ached, watching the suffering of those we love and care about. And yet we have become masterful at building walls to defend us from love, holding on to grievances, and protecting our hearts from a moment of truth, or from someone who might touch us too deeply.

THE SOURCE OF ALL HEALING

There are three basic directions that love can flow and three basic questions we can ask in every moment to determine the awakened status of our heart. They are:

- *Love of self*—"In this moment, do I genuinely love myself?"

- *Love of another*—"In this moment, how am I expressing my love to someone else?"

- *The ability to receive love*—"In this moment, am I worthy of love?"

The *Sacred Power of Your Awakened Heart* holds the key to your divine magnificence. Your ability to see yourself in the hearts of others, feel worthy of love, and hold another person's heart in your own, is what we learn as we walk the Fifth Divine Path. When your heart is truly "awakened," it is the most powerful, expansive, and transformational aspect of your being. In this divine state of *bodhicitta*, you can effortlessly give and receive love, flow gratitude, step beyond fear, awaken your purpose, and experience joy in each moment.

THE AWAKENED HEART KNOWS ALL

When storm clouds seem to overtake your emotions; when you find yourself feeling shame, jealousy, self-doubt, inadequacy, or loneliness; when the shield of pride you constantly hold up to protect yourself has become too heavy, your *awakened heart* is there to comfort and heal you. Those moments of anger, arrogance, judgment, and condescension, where you brandish a sword of self-importance to demonstrate your strength, power, or confidence, your *awakened heart* knows this is simply a defensive ploy to attack the world and distract yourself from the tender hurt oozing from the center of your heart-puddle.

Your awakened heart knows all, sees all, feels all, and is capable of healing all the pain and suffering that rests inside you. And in its boundless wisdom, your awakened heart can deliver an ever-expanding wholeness to your every thought, word, and action. The pathway to this higher state of existence is through living each moment from that sacred space of love to be divinely guided to fulfill your heart's desires, summon the courage to take your life to the next level, and discover your meaning in life.

CHAPTER TWENTY-SIX

THE 10 AWAKENINGS OF THE HEART

When you master the art of being fully awake
to this moment, you bestow a precious gift
on your soul—the experience of love.

— Debbie Ford

LETTING LOVE FLOW

Love starts the moment we listen to our heart, which never lies. Our intellect may misinterpret what our heart speaks to us—but the heart never—ever—lies. It is pure, whole perfect, and enlightened. Which is why it is so important to spend time in stillness and silence, to allow our inner essence to get so quiet that we hear the divine whispers of our heart. Throughout our lives, we have navigated many different types of love, from the love of our parents, teachers, and best friends to schoolmate crushes, romantic moments, and passionate sharing, to the love of animals, our children, and our life partner to the love of Spirit, the Divine, and God.

The more we know about how love grows, builds, and evolves, the more easily we can give and receive it—and the more it will fill our life. Remember, where attention goes, energy flows. Witnessing the progressive expansion of love as it moves through the stages of awareness, then attraction, then understanding, and ultimately into one-ness is an important key to our self-awareness and our ability to feel love. All love follows this basic path as it is cultivated. And yet there is an even deeper, more subtle progression of how the heart awakens its sacred power.

IN A PAST LIFE

According to the Nadi, 3,000 years ago, in one of my past lives, I was trained by the masters of timeless wisdom to walk the *Divine Path of Inner Fire*. He revealed that I was a student of the Awakened Heart and had spent many years studying under several enlightened seers, including an Indian female philosopher known as Ghosha. According to the Nadi, her body was riddled with leprosy and so she was mostly confined to her father's house. But for some reason, I befriended her, and for several years, together we studied the teachings of *Bhakti* (devotional sacred love). She trained me in the wisdom of the *Divine Principle of Inner Fire*, specifically the *Sacred Power of the Awakened Heart*.

I began formally sharing this wisdom with others throughout the kingdom. She was immersed so deeply into her practice that ultimately it healed her. And shortly after, I was killed by one of her suitors. She then married and had a child. That was lifetimes ago. So, let me now share with you these sacred teachings of love that flow through me, and you can apply them to your life.

LOVE EVOLUTION

One of the core aspects of the *Sacred Power of the Awakened Heart* is that love evolves divinely through 10 naturally unfolding states called *the 10 Awakenings of the Heart*. As your awareness of these 10 states of love grows, your heart begins to reveal itself as a sacred instrument for profound healing, personal empowerment, sweet rapture, deeper fulfillment, and spiritual enlightenment. Simply reading all 10, and seeing how they apply to your life, will powerfully shift your feelings about love and begin a deep self-reflection on all of your relationships. This is a critical starting point for awakening your heart.

Once you understand these 10 states of love at an energetic level, you can recognize which state you are experiencing in any given moment. And, from this space of expanded awareness, you can nourish the *Sacred Power of Your Awakened Heart* and flow its best expression into your life to love more deeply, receive its tenderness, and make divinely inspired, heart-based decisions. The *10 Awakenings of the Heart* unfold progressively like this:

1. Listening

You can receive the world through your heart. You need to get real still . . . real silent . . . real calm . . . and in the quietude of that moment, you will hear the Universe speaking to you. You can't multitask while you do this; you need to cut through all the other noise that's swirling around you. We call it listening but it's actually the act of *divine receiving*—it's passively calling in the sacred and allowing all of your senses to function through your heart. Try it. Right now, close your eyes and truly see with your heart—envision that your heart has the ability to perceive in the physical realm, to observe in the emotional realm and to witness in the spiritual realm. Allow your heart to hear any voices or whispers being transmitted at the frequency of your heart.

Right now, invite someone into your heart. This can be anyone: someone you deeply love or loved; someone you desire; someone you are missing; someone who was once there for you or who you were once there for; someone who has passed on; the child you once were; a companion animal who once shared your heart. Now place your hand or rest the tips of your fingers on your heart, close your eyes, and let the vibration come into you—what are you truly feeling? Speak the words that you feel. First silently . . . then whisper them . . . then say them out loud, "I feel _____." Keep listening as you connect more deeply with your emotions. When we get still and silent, we can hear the whispers of the Divine coming through our hearts. Stay in this space for as long as you like—and use this powerful tool of heart listening throughout the day. This is the very first state of love; listening is the spark of all love. And without it, no love can blossom.

2. Attraction

We all know it. We feel it not just in our heart, but in various places throughout our body. Some people refer to it as charm—others call it magnetism. It's the moment we start to pay attention to someone or something with a desire to keep paying attention. We are often attracted to traits, characteristics, or aspects of others that we wish we had more of. We then develop a bit of an attachment to that trait through that person. We are inspired by another's courage, peacefulness, passion, integrity, or kindness because we recognize a hint of that trait in ourselves and we desire its awakening.

You can tell that you are attracted to someone because their face, their words, and their energy hold your attention and you begin to cultivate an attachment. Right now, you can detect your current attachments. From a quiet state of listening, ask yourself, "What am I drawn to? Where does my mind keep settling? What desires seem to arise from this space? How does it make me feel? Who am I attracted to?" We can be attracted to people or things that don't nourish us as well as those that are life-affirming. Attraction is more of a heightened state of attention infused with a growing attachment, and it is often a one-way flow of energy. This is where we often believe that we "like" someone or something because they make us feel good in some way—we like their *energy*. Who comes into your awareness when you ask, "Who am I attracted to?" And how intense is that attraction on a scale of 1 to 10?

3. Fascination

As we become more attached to the shiny object of our attention, it starts to become the *only* object of our attention, and the result is *fascination*. Often referred to as infatuation, fascination is a deepening state of attraction in which our involuntary attachment to a person or thing becomes all-consuming. Some psychology researchers call this phenomena *limerence*. As fascination builds, we become captivated by unfamiliar, new, or pleasurable feelings that hijack our attention and heighten the intensity of the attachment. We become single-minded in our quest to prolong the experience and our brain begins to flood with a powerful combination of four feel-good chemicals—dopamine (heightening our anticipation of a reward), oxytocin (nourishing our reward pathways and increasing our desire for social bonding), endorphin (masking our pain), and serotonin (elevating our mood).

Is it Love? Or Just Chemicals?

As our focus narrows on the object of our attention, our fascination intensifies and can even take the form of obsession. This is a common emotional expression in online flirtations, affairs, and brand-new relationships with people, places, or situations, and can often include transference—the unconscious redirection of feelings we have for another person such as a parent, spouse, or ex. In *fascination transference*, we attribute all the positive qualities of someone onto the object of our fascination and ascribe them none of the negative qualities, which makes them super attractive. Modern science has confirmed that hormones and chemicals produced and released into the environment by both men and women can influence the behavior and physiology of others. And this is certainly true for those in a state of fascination. In our chemically induced intoxication, we fasten on to one "fascinating" aspect of the person and we let all other characteristics fade into the background.

In many cases, fascination is a way to fill an emotional emptiness within us. In our fascination, we start to fantasize ourselves being with the other person or thing in all sorts of situations. We project what the future will look like with us embedded in our "new" life, and either daydream about or discuss fantasy-world scenarios. And although there is often a heightened sexual tension or physical component at this level of attraction, the environment where fascination occurs can be work based, team based, project oriented, home related, and even recreational. In this state of love, we are often blind to any negative information the other person has shared, or obvious red-flag signals that others may see. We may even ignore physical traits that we don't find attractive because we are laser focused on the one "fascinating" aspect of the person.

Running Out of Fuel

After racing at a fevered pitch for days, weeks, and in some cases months, fascination peaks, culminating in a chemical and emotional crescendo. Incapable of sustaining such an extreme level of intensity, the nonstop intoxication ultimately gives way to exhaustion, as the influence of hormones and chemicals weakens and the seductive power of the unfamiliar gives way to the familiar. As our sober mind takes back its traditional position of rational decision maker, our fantasy of a perfect person or ideal scenario fades. Soon, previously invisible flaws, negative attributes, and imperfections come to light and as the bigger picture unfolds, our fascination wanes. Are you in a relationship now with anyone or anything where your level of fascination is beginning to wane?

Two Paths Out of Fascination

From the state of fascination, you can move in one of two directions. Our infatuation softens, and we begin accepting the pros and the cons of the object of our fascination—allowing our love to grow deeper beyond all the bells and whistles that once wowed us. Or, in some cases, a sense of shame for being so "foolish" or "blind" makes us reject the object of our fascination and a sense of aversion replaces our sense of attachment. Often, from this state of "dislike," we suppress the emotions we had and vow never to let ourselves "feel" that deeply ever again. Have you moved on from any person or object of fascination and found yourself either loving them more deeply or rejecting them? How have you shifted the way you "listen" to love?

What If My Heart Breaks?

If you've found yourself saddened by the emotions you once held so dearly, and you have begun to deny those emotions—this is you creating a wall around your heart, planting seeds of bitterness, foolishness, self-judgment, and massive transference. You begin painting the world with your shame, resentment, and hostility. This is where you need to remember that the tenderest part of you is also the strongest part of you. And in your vulnerability rests your strength, if you are willing to go there. Each of us has had their heart broken; you've had yours broken, and I've had mine broken. And most likely, we've both broken someone else's as well. How does heartbreak happen? We trust someone or something so completely—and then that trust is removed, lost, or turned on its head. And, what we do in response to that heartbreak determines the depth of our wound and its ability to heal.

At the moment our heart is broken, there is not a brilliant adviser on staff telling us what we should do—and even if there was, most likely we're in no condition to listen. What we decide to do will be our heart's defining moment. *There is only one step to emotional freedom*—only one step that will allow you to love again and that is self-kindness and empathy. You must decide right now that you are worthy of the love of the Universe—and that you certainly are worthy of being loved again by another. If you make the commitment right now to self-love and empathy, the hardening of your heart will stop . . . a softening will occur . . . and love will begin showing up on your doorstep.

4. Empathy

The first step in shifting a relationship from one of attraction to one of understanding occurs when we expand our view beyond our own emotions and begin a bilateral connection process that takes into account how another person feels. The most direct path to that place is the state of empathy where we can place ourselves into the shoes of another person and feel as if we genuinely "know" the depth of *their* emotion, not simply our own. When we empathize, we authentically "experience" the other's pain in our own heart. This is more than a touchy-feely state. Science has actually discovered "mirror neurons" that react to the complex emotions of others and then internalize them as our own. And, yes, oxytocin, the chemical of bonding, plays a key role in this process.

Taking Love to the Next Level

Empathy is a deeper state of understanding than sympathy, which is having a sense of regret regarding another person's pain. Empathy, on the other hand, is when you understand and truly feel the other person's feelings as your own. Empathy has more depth than attraction or fascination because in this state, energy seems to flow both to us and from us as we delve into the other person's heart.

Why Should I Forgive?

You can be attracted to an inanimate object and you can be fascinated with a beach resort, but empathy is an energetic sharing of emotion. And that takes love to another level. Empathy is an important starting point to forgiveness. We can forgive more easily when we can see ourselves in the shoes of the other person and feel we understand what might have been in another person's heart—the intention behind their action. *When we forgive, we free ourselves*; it doesn't mean we accept, condone, excuse, or pardon the hurtful behavior. *When we forgive, we are simply letting go of our attachment to our victimhood* and the negative emotions associated with it such as our need for revenge or justice. These toxic emotions can consume people's lives forever, hardening their own hearts while the other person moves on and forgets they even broke a heart.

Empathy of Self

Empathy is the doorway to true love because all love begins with self-love. And only when we having kindness for our own plight can we extend that authentic kindness to others. The ancient wisdom traditions teach us that the starting point for all healing is first accepting who we are at our very core. This empathy of self is one of the most elusive teachings for us to grasp because humans are their own harshest critics. We have always criticized and scolded ourselves for our weaknesses, mistakes, and errors in judgment. And a lifetime of that can certainly obscure the possibility of self-forgiveness. But that's where we need to begin—recognizing how harsh and judgmental we have been to ourselves for every imperfection of our naturally imperfect humanity.

True Empathy Is Pure Understanding

There is no finger wagging in empathy. There is no condescension. No scolding or trying to teach a lesson. There is no blame or fault.

There is only understanding—understanding that it is human to have emotions of pain, sorrow, shame, guilt, or sadness. *We realize that we are not the emotion; but rather, that we are experiencing the emotion.* In this deep understanding, we see the regret, the grief, the anguish, and the desperation for what it was and what it is—feeling it in the depths of our being and showering it with loving-kindness. And so this journey of deep uncontrived understanding for all those in pain begins with understanding the pain in our own heart, and taking the critical step of forgiving our self for loving and trusting so deeply—which in turn, we will realize, is actually a cause for celebration. This is the moment where you realize that your sensitivity is one of the most special traits the Universe could ever gift you. The next time someone tells you that you are too sensitive, thank them for giving you such an amazing compliment.

5. Compassion

The moment our empathy deepens from feeling someone else's pain in our own heart to a more expansive state *of rooting for that suffering to end*—it becomes compassion. That is because true compassion is the state where we are literally "moved" into love—where the *Sacred Power of Your Awakened Heart* is activated as an instrument of healing. The ancient origin of the word comes from two Latin words *compassio*, meaning "fellow feeling," and *compati*, meaning "to suffer with." Empathy acknowledges the "you" in "me," compassion takes it deeper by recognizing the "me" in "you"—where *your pain IS my pain*. The truly awakened heart not only understands the depth of someone else's pain but is also willing to actually bear that pain. An old song, "He Ain't Heavy, He's My Brother," speaks eloquently to the powerful dynamic contained in compassion.

The Ultimate Commitment

Compassion is a state of love, yet it's often misunderstood and confused with other emotions. True compassion is the ability to be sympathetic, empathetic, *as well as having the desire to alleviate another's pain and suffering,* and in its most profound form also includes *the willingness to take on the burden of that pain.* Compassion goes far beyond the teaching of the Golden Rule: "Do unto others as you would have others do unto you." Compassion is a state of unconditional love that is more akin to the biblical verse "Love your neighbor as yourself." There may be people in our life that we like, even love, yet the depth of our compassion for them is shallow. Perhaps fear, jealousy, resentment, guilt, anger, or laziness prevent us from loving them unconditionally. The secret to flowing the *Sacred Power of Your Awakened Heart* as you move throughout the day is to commit to compassion—self-compassion and compassion for others. An easy starting point is when you find yourself in moments of judgment, harshness, or self-absorption, gently remind yourself, "I see myself in the other and the other in myself."

True Compassion
How can we know if we are feeling compassion about something and are not simply attached? Remember that true compassion is independent of attachment; it is unconditional. Imagine if our compassion could transcend our relationships and the attachment we have to them—pure sympathy, pure empathy, and pure desire to help them heal. It is the ultimate characteristic of emotional intelligence.

But we need to remember that all compassion starts with self-compassion. If you are not rooting for yourself in each moment, how can you root for others? If you can't empathize with your own plight and root for your own suffering to end, then your heart is not truly awakened. And it's from the depths of our own heart that compassion is birthed. Healing others begins with healing yourself. Right now, in this moment, can you commit to more self-compassion? Is there something in your life—some action you took, some words you spoke, some thoughts you held tightly, that you could give yourself permission to forgive? Can you forgive yourself right now for being so hard on yourself?

6. Selfless Care

The compassion that we awaken when we experience someone suffering can be taken to an even deeper state of love when offered proactively instead of reactively—not just in response to someone obviously in distress, but without any conditions or contingencies. This state of love, also known as *divine affection*, transcends compassion in that it flows unconditionally from an awakened heart *all the time*—not simply when we sense pain or where suffering is noticeable. We see it in the around-the-clock selfless care we give to a baby, a pet, a child, or someone in a weakened, handicapped, or innocent state.

This state of love is awakened when we give selflessly with no expectation of a thank-you; when we offer our love with no conditions; when we shower our own heart with love simply because we can; when we give a gift anonymously; or do something special for someone that they most likely won't even notice. Selfless care comes from a deep space in *Your Awakened Heart* that requires no trigger—only the deep desire to raise the vibration of love in another being. It flows as effortlessly as breath, and does not require that it be received or responded to in any expected way. You will know this state of love has arrived in your life, when you awaken each morning, with the excitement that you get to radiate selfless care.

7. Divine Friendship

When the exchange of selfless care flows two ways without any score keeping, you have evolved to this state of love. Also referred to as *communion*, in the state of Divine Friendship two awakened hearts beat as one. Built on an understanding of wholeness and a belief in the *Sacred Power of Abundance*, in Divine Friendship both awakened hearts are in recognition that their combined love will always equal more than the whole. This requires unconditional trust that there will be an ever-flowing current of love passing back and forth between the two. When one person is weak, the other is strong and vice versa.

Divine Friendship evolves over time, as trust builds. In this state of love, each person interacts with the same grace and ease as your right hand and your left hand—they can work independently or together, but they never work against each other. Their trust in each other is pure, unwavering, unconditional, and free of judgment. This state of love can exist in the workplace as well as in the home as the awakened hearts of Divine Friendship are always rooting for each other to succeed.

8. Pure Surrender

As the practice of this heart-based communion evolves even further, a state of love unfolds rooted in unconditional vulnerability and defenselessness. In this state of love, you fully surrender to the Divine and trust in the Universe unconditionally. Whatever happens in your life, good or bad, you rarely ask, "Why me?" In fact, you don't see the world as good or bad—each moment is simply an experience to learn and grow from. You absorb the pain and suffering of everyone around you, and flow back only love because your awakened heart has finally become a conduit for deeper healing inside and healing all those around you who suffer.

Trusting the Universe

The truly awakened heart is upheld by the *Divine Principle of Infinite Flow*, in which it is fully surrendered—trusting so completely that it no longer needs any protection. The awakened heart in a state of Pure Surrender accepts that this moment is perfect; no longer clings to any concerns of the past; and fully embraces the present moment. With no fear of the future, and fully released from any past-laden grievances, this state of love is pure and defenseless, willing to die to the past in every moment, and released from all constrictions. This is the highest state of love that can realistically be attained by most of us.

When two people share this merged awakened heart, they both believe in the core of their very being that the Universe will tenderly cradle them in the sacred shelter of their divine friendship. This allows the most intimate state of love—filled with innocence, openness, honesty, and complete transparency. The fully surrendered awakened heart is beyond the emotions of embarrassment, humiliation, shame, or guilt. Vulnerability drives each moment as both awakened hearts merge together into the true tenderness of love. This is the most passionate love that humans can experience—because you are an instrument of the Divine fueled by the energy of the Universe.

9. Divine Gratitude

When surrender is so complete, the awakened heart evolves even more deeply to a state of Divine Gratitude. In this state of love, no matter what unfolds, you are grateful. Whatever you receive, you understand it as a generous gift from the Universe. You are beyond fear or sadness because you realize that the Universe, God, or your Higher Power is directing the course of events; and you are a surrendered passenger who can only marvel at the journey. In the wake of the most startling news—a diagnosis, a death, a divorce—you are appreciative that you have been gifted with a huge, awakened heart that can absorb it all, hold space for others, bear the burdens of life, melt them, and continue on with grace. The ancient teachings refer to this state of love as *enlightened love*, and for most of us, it is simply an ideal state to which we can aspire but never actually achieve on a sustained basis.

This is a highly evolved state and living in it full time is reserved for only the most awakened beings who have ever walked the earth—nameless saints, unknown martyrs, timeless prophets, and the miscellaneous handful of anonymous souls who have experienced this gift. They are not activists and they have no cause to proclaim other than tender healing. They seek no fame, no material riches. We don't see them on TV or in videos. They're not on social media, and they don't draw attention to themselves. They are here only to relieve the suffering of others, bear their burdens, and ease their pain. In this state of love, there is no karma.

Nothing can stain their heart. Nothing can taint their belief. They are perfect in their human imperfection. Saint Mother Teresa lived her life in Divine Gratitude, selflessly giving her heart in every moment to serve the wishes of the Divine.

The ancient teachings sometimes referred to these people as *enlightened bodhisattvas*—those who had become enlightened during their lifetime, and yet had chosen to stay here on earth helping those in pain, rather than leaving their body and experiencing the eternal bliss of nirvana. They are the physical embodiment of divine love—and as such, they are the perfect ideal for us to aspire to. In this state of love, every moment is heaven on earth. When you arrive at this state of love, you realize that you have been selected by the Universe to serve in this life at the highest level—and recognition of this gift keeps you in a state of constant awe, the deepest fulfillment, and eternal gratitude until you are asked to leave.

10. Miraculous Love

The ability to act as an egoless human expression of the Divine has been gifted to only a few since time began. Jesus maintained that he was not God; Buddha requested that he not be celebrated after his death. Yet, more than 2,000 years later, their essences and their energies ripple throughout the lives of billions of earthlings. Miraculous Love transcends space and time—and we are the receivers of it in every moment. We feel it when the wind blows, when thunder cracks, when the nightingale sings, and when the sun sets. We experience it with every breath we take and in every beat of our heart. When we feel heaven on earth, we are experiencing a tiny spark of the boundless, infinite, brilliance of Miraculous Love. When we drift into the one-ness of existence during meditation, we glimpse a flicker of the most magnificent love that could ever exist.

Awakening Love

Miraculous Love is showering you right now, flowing effortlessly into your awakened heart. Yet some of us are still searching for it around every corner. When you look outside yourself for any kind of love, you are sure to miss it or find something else disguised as love. But, now that you understand that all love flows from self-love, you have an opportunity to shift your entire life and live it purely and miraculously from the inside out.

Through the daily practices of self-kindness, self-forgiveness, self-compassion, and self-love, the *Sacred Power of Your Awakened Heart* will bring you the healing, transformation, and deep loving you so desire.

CHAPTER TWENTY-SEVEN

THE SACRED POWER
OF PASSION

A mighty flame followeth a tiny spark.

— Dante Alighieri

The *Divine Principle of Inner Fire* is burning within you right now. When you ask yourself, "What does my heart truly long for?"— even if you think you don't know—if you allow yourself to get still, you do hear the answers. And that voice inside of you that's whispering what it so deeply desires is the voice of your *Sacred Power of Passion*. And although the whispers may come from your heart, the answers are actually formed in a place a bit lower on your torso known as the solar plexus. *Plexus* is the Latin word for "intersection," and this sacred place below your rib cage and behind your diaphragm is where a core network of nerves branch out in a pattern mimicking the sun, hence the word *solar*. Essentially this is the intersection of the sun and your belly. This is where that primordial supernova explosion that sparked the entire creation of the Universe now rests inside of you. It is in your personal sun in the center of your body.

HEAT AND LIGHT

Place your hand on this space right now, right in the center of your chest and a few inches below your breastbone. You can feel it. It's the place where your passion resides; where the fire inside you burns; and where your desires transform into action. For passion to unfold in a sacred and divine expression, you will require just the right amount of light and just the right amount of heat. Too much light without heat brings attention *but no intention*, a state of passionless clarity. Too much heat without light brings unfocused intensity, a state of passionate darkness. Reflect on your last interaction with someone. Did you bring more light or more heat to the situation? Did you illuminate or leave the sting of a burn?

THE POWER OF YOUR DIGESTIVE FIRE

The *Divine Principle of Inner Fire* is one of ingestion, digestion, and expression. The Universe flows into us, we chew on it a bit, we absorb what serves us, we let go of what doesn't, and then we flow what remains back out. Every moment is one of dynamic exchange. There is an ancient Indian concept known as *Agni*, the Sanskrit word for digestive fire. We get the English words *ignite* and *ignition* from this 7,000-year old word. The premise of Agni is that if your digestive fire is burning brightly at the perfect temperature, it will ingest all it receives, digest all the nourishment, and leave behind sweet, vital nectar known as *ojas*, pronounced oh-jas. If the fire is burning too hot or is sputtering and not burning hot enough, it won't cook what it receives and it will leave behind toxic residue known in Sanskrit as *ama*. We are reminded of this process every time we eat something. We've all had the meal that puts us to sleep or bloats us. And we've all had the meal that leaves us feeling uplifted and satisfied. Every moment is one of ojas or ama.

OJAS OR AMA?

Just like our physical digestive system ingests, digests, and eliminates, the *Divine Principle of Inner Fire* teaches us that our emotional digestive fire impacts all of our experiences. For example, we "chew" on a conversation or interaction with our senses; we "break it down" with our intellect; we take in the words, the tone, the intent, and the sentiment; and then depending how brightly our emotional Agni is burning, we digest it, absorbing all the aspects of the interaction that we believe will serve us and releasing that which has no further use.

What determines whether we leave behind ojas or ama in a given moment? It depends on the following three cultivations:

1. How openly we receive the information—without coloring it with our constrictions—our judgments, prejudices, opinions, preconceived notions, and arrogance.

2. How mindful we are to the present moment—our ability to patiently listen, let someone finish their sentences, observe the rise and fall of their breath, watch their facial expressions, gaze lovingly into their eyes, and not drift into the past or the future.

3. How curious, innocent, and vulnerable we can risk being—our willingness to allow the unknown to unfold without energizing fear, mistrust, suspicion, manipulation, or any of our protective masks.

If our fire is burning brightly, we trust, we listen, we stay fully present, and we risk being vulnerable. And, ideally, once we have absorbed all that we believe will nourish us, we release, sidestep, or let go of anything that will not serve us. If our emotional digestive fire is burning brightly, we don't take on any extra baggage from the interaction, such as regrets or grievances. When we put our head on the pillow at night, there is no ama that follows us into our dreams—only pure ojas.

So again, reflect on your last interaction with someone. Did you leave behind *ojas* (sweet vital nectar) or *ama* (toxic residue)? Did you destroy the best of your intentions because an emotional delivery of your words got in the way? Or did your words have greater impact because you flowed the perfect amount of heat?

A DELICATE BALANCE

Brilliant ideas can be undermined by poor execution. Expressing yourself effectively is that magnificent balance of light and heat. Important needs can remain unmet, leaving turbulence in their wake, because they were stated with harshness rather than kindness. When we passionately exaggerate, it weakens the validity of our cause. And when we dispassionately mumble our desires, they are not taken seriously. As we walk this *Fifth Divine Path of Transformation*, the results we achieve depend wholly on how we moderate heat and light, balancing the focus of our attention and the intensity of our intention. Right now, with your hand still resting on your solar plexus, ask yourself, "Is there more light or more heat rising up from within me?" Let this be the eternal barometer of the effectiveness of your words and actions. Feel you own internal fire. And after every encounter, remember to ask yourself, "Did I just leave *ojas* (sweet vital nectar) or *ama* (toxic residue) behind?" Only when your heart is awakened can you hear the voice of deep desire speaking truth with heat *and* light, which is why the process of awakening our heart is so important to the *Sacred Power of Passion*.

For thousands of years, the ancient wisdom traditions have referred to this location as the *manipura*, which can be translated as "the city of jewels." And, throughout time, the manipura was considered the true fire center of our being—the place where our desires, dreams, intentions, and determination all merged into an energetic expression of who we are. Based on the power of this convergence in any given moment, this divine force of nature ebbs and flows, rises and falls, sleeps and rages, just as any fire can adjust from a faint flicker to an all-consuming blaze.

When the fire is weak, our resolve is weak. When the fire is strong, we are on a mission where there is little we are unwilling to undertake.

YOUR MOST AUTHENTIC PLACE

Once you awakened the *Sacred Power of Attention* in your life, this began your ever-expanding journey toward clarity. We are always polishing the mirror so we can see our reflection more clearly. We've spent a lot of time on "owning" where we've come from and acknowledging who we *were*. From the *Divine Formula* to the *Shakti Manifestation*, many of the exercises we've explored together are designed to gently navigate us from looking through our rearview mirror to a place of authentically seeing ourselves in the now. So, let's start where you are right now, with your current level of comfort, which will only build as you continue to walk the path.

The *Sacred Power of Release* teaches us that fire has a powerful ability to burn away that which no longer serves us. The *Sacred Power of Passion* has distilling properties as well, but even more important is its ability to focus, fuse, and channel heat in the direction of a target. Passion has an endgame: the achievement of your desire. And in its quest to fulfill those desires, passion becomes single-minded, concentrating its light on the object of its attention and leaving in darkness all lower priorities.

NOURISHMENT OR DISTRACTION?

As it burns through the haze, powering past all the shiny objects around it that would hijack your attention, passion asks the question in every moment, "Nourishment or distraction?" It keeps you grounded and on track. It keeps you leaning in the direction of your desire. Passion stands unwavering at the finish line, cheering for you to put one foot in front of the other, stay the course, and let your momentum carry you. And it doesn't let up until you tell it to, which is why keeping the fire burning is so critical to the fulfillment of your goals.

MOMENTUM AND ACCELERATION

Comfort leads to confidence, which leads to courage, which then leads to action, which is the starting point for transformation. When we are comfortable with who we believe we are, we walk through the world effortlessly. This allows us to show up, test the waters, dip our toe in, and begin the process of wading into the shallow end. Once we realize the water's not too cold, we give ourselves permission to move forward into the depths. It is from this sacred space that confidence is born. And through the *Sacred Power of Passion*, momentum turns into acceleration. We put our foot on the gas and never look back.

PASSION BLOSSOMS AT THE EDGE OF YOUR COMFORT ZONE

In the past, when you have faltered at this critical moment, it is because you began second-guessing yourself. You allowed your self-confidence to be challenged because your inner fire had flickered a little bit. You stopped trusting in the *Divine Principle* that had stoked your passion. The reality is that momentum ebbs and flows. When it throttles back for any reason, you need to step in for just a moment, tap the gas, and keep moving forward. Push through the edge of your comfort zone and establish a new one. This can be a do-or-die moment in the achievement of your dreams, a moment you have visited many times before.

So, in this pause that the Universe has generously gifted you, with the divine opportunity to back off, freeze, or leap, this is where you double-down, step into your power, lean in to your conviction just a little bit harder, and put your foot firmly down on the accelerator of your inner fire. This is the defining moment where the *Sacred Power of Passion* whispers three transformational questions that have the potential to shift your life forever: "What's your deepest desire?" "Why is it important?" and "How much do you want it?" Whatever you answer then takes on a life of its own. This is where you get the chance to choose *you*. This is the moment of truth, where you break the cycle that has held you back forever, step into your best version, and officially announce, *"I choose me!"* And in that moment of conscious choice making, the perseverance of your manipura keeps you focused on the prize. Acceleration begins again, your momentum reengages, and your passion center is infused with confidence. This is where courage begins to awaken.

AWAKENING THE VIRTUE OF COURAGE

Courage is your ability to do something that frightens you because you have found the strength to power through fear, pain, or grief. The *Sacred Power of Your Awakened Heart* is built on divine love and unconditional trust, which allows you to transcend fear in any moment. Once you are firmly established in this state, you have created the important foundation for you to awaken the *Sacred Power of Your Passion*, which is a force of nature. When the divine light of your manipura (shining brightly and fueled with the fortitude of laser focus) meets the miraculous love of your awakened heart (trusting completely in the unconditional support of the Universe), courage arises naturally.

Courage is a virtue. And like the virtues of patience and justice, a person must be able to sustain courage in the face of difficulty or adversity. You know how challenging it can be to maintain patience when someone is pressuring you, or to stand in your truth when others are pushing you to adopt a contrary belief. These are virtues because they need to be cultivated, nourished, and practiced no matter what the outside world is telling you.

Awakening the *Virtue of Courage* requires heart *and* fortitude—the willingness to hold your feet to the fire because you trust that the Universe will deliver you to exactly where you need to be. Courage blossoms from the merging of the *Sacred Power of the Awakened Heart* and the *Sacred Power of Passion*, because transcending your fear of the unknown requires a depth of unconditional trust. Courage is based on the eighth state of love—surrender—which states:

The awakened heart in a state of surrender accepts that this moment is perfect, no longer clings to any concerns of the past, and fully embraces the present moment. With no fear of the future, and fully released from any past-laden grievances, this state of love is pure and defenseless, willing to die to the past in every moment, and released from all constrictions. This is the highest state of love that can truly be attained by any of us.

AWAKENING COURAGE

Courage has three distinct expressions. We can cultivate our sense of *physical courage*—fortifying our belief that our body is whole and strong and capable of doing more, trying more, and getting more done. We can cultivate our *emotional courage* by not taking things personally, feeling worthy, and fortifying our ability to reach outside of our comfort zone. And we can cultivate our sense of *moral courage* by not listening to all the contrary voices around us, going deeper into our shining light, and standing up for what we "know" is right, fair, and just. Martin Luther King, Jr., a powerful archetype for the *Divine Principle of Inner Fire*, described his manipura breakthrough moment with the words, "I moved to break the betrayal of my own silences and to speak from the burnings of my own heart." He was able to harness, focus, and channel his rage into transformational, nonviolent action.

Courage is awakened in that sliver of a moment where we decide to act. Where the flame in you meets the eternal fire of the Universe and you become grounded in your belief that you will take the fearless step in spite of everything around you telling you to fear. The *Sacred Power of Passion* is there to light your way as you step boldly into your power.

So let's see where that leads you right now. For this exercise, you'll need to find some quiet space and a pen to begin moving what's in your body and mind into the tangible world outside your physical form. Follow the steps, or feel free to use a separate piece of paper for the *Awakening My Passion* process:

Awakening My Passion

1. What is my deepest driving desire? Right now, what does my heart long for?

_____

_____

_____

_____

_____

2. Why is this important to me? Why do I care?

_____

_____

_____

_____

3. How much do I truly want it? (Answer on a scale of 1–10, where 1 is not at all, and 10 is more than anything in life.)

_____

_____

_____

_____

_____

The answer to Question 3 is the best determinant of your level of passion. If you answered with a rating lower than 8, then your passion index is weak. Don't despair. That might be because you didn't go deep enough regarding your desire, or because you are trying to accomplish too many other things that are distracting you.

BREAKING THROUGH THE CLOUDS

But don't fret. This next exercise is designed to tease some passion out of you. We'll take it even deeper and light the flame of passion more brightly by crystalizing a core element of the manipura: *your ability to follow through*. Imagine that there is a sun in the center of your solar plexus. Your inner sun is always shining brightly but you have allowed a whole bunch of clouds to pass between the burning rays inside of you and the brilliant energy of transformation that is shining outside of you. For passion to awaken and achievement of your goal to occur, those two lights must converge to become one.

What do the clouds in front of your sun look like? Are they thin and wispy? Or thick and heavy? Are they dark or light? Are they filled with rain or air? Get clear on your clouds and begin to radiate the sun from your solar plexus to burn them away. Place your hand on your manipura, and go deeper into the visualization.

What are your clouds made of? Excuses? Laziness? Memories of past failure? A limiting belief? Or a sense of fear over making a shift? By drilling deep into the answers to these questions, you will start to transcend your blockages. We can do this by simply answering the 10 questions of the *Breaking through the Clouds Exercise.*

Breaking through the Clouds Exercise

1. What's a current issue or disturbance that is challenging me right now?

   _____

   _____

2. What is the impact that this issue or disturbance is creating in my physical life?

   _____

   _____

3. What is the impact that this issue or disturbance is creating in my emotional state?

   _____

   _____

4. What is the impact that this issue or disturbance is creating in my material world?

   _____

   _____

5. What is the impact that this issue or disturbance is creating in my relationships?

   _____

   _____

6. What is the impact that this issue or disturbance is creating in my spiritual life?

    _____

    _____

7. What happens if I do nothing?

    _____

    _____

8. What would I like to see unfold?

    _____

    _____

9. What are the top three characteristics, core traits, skill sets, or strengths that will best move me through this challenge?

    _____

    _____

10. How brightly am I willing to shine my inner sun to break through the clouds?

    _____

    _____

Pretty powerful. Right? But, let's go even deeper.

WAKING UP THE GODS AND GODDESSES

This next phase of walking the *Divine Path of Inner Fire* will further stoke the embers of your passion, as we explore an ancient practice known as *Awakening the Divine*. This teaching has its beginnings in the 7,000-year-old teachings of the ancient Indian text the Rig Veda, yet it can be applied to your life right now. Whenever you are just about to leap out of one aspect of your life and into another—a job, a relationship, a belief system, or a new beginning—sometimes we can feel like we don't have the energy, confidence, courage, or smarts to take us to the next level. Sometimes it's a little voice in our head telling us we can't do it, a person in our life shaking their head or smirking, or simply daunting circumstances. This is pretty common. So when we realize that we don't have what it takes in the critical moment, don't give up. Instead simply reach for an *archetype.*

An archetype is the embodiment in another being, mythical character, or force of nature that contains a core trait, skill set, characteristic, or strength that we need to draw upon in the critical moment. An easy archetype to understand might be if you have to lift a heavy object, let's say moving a big box from one room to another. In that moment, you would probably call on someone who is very strong or capable of lifting heavy weights. Not by dialing the phone or sending an e-mail but instead by connecting to an archetype. You'd summon whomever you think of when you think of pure physical strength. In this instance, I would awaken my inner Hulk, connect with that powerful Hulk energy deep in my core, and move those boxes. Done!

CALLING IN YOUR STRENGTH

Archetypes are inner states of information, energy, and awareness that are sleeping inside us. By awakening them, we summon the divine power of the Universe in finding our next gear. Archetypes exist in the collective domain of the unmanifest and are available to each of us at any time through the *Sacred Power of Passion*. They exist as a god or goddess curled up inside you waiting to be born. And they can take the form or shape of whatever it is we are trying to summon. Simply pick a trait and think of someone over the course of your life who embodies it. Creativity? Michelangelo. Compassion? The Dalai Lama. Standing your ground? Rosa Parks. Stepping into your power? Wonder Woman. (Yes. Superheroes and She-roes are brilliant archetypes.) You can choose an element in nature such as the sun or the wind; someone in your life who has embodied these traits; an inspirational figure; or a famous being in history you admire.

Once we are clear on who they are, we can trigger our archetypes in any moment and awaken them simply by planting the seeds of our intentions and desires in that radiating inner sun of our manipura. If we practice this process of *Awakening the Divine* on a regular basis, we get more skilled at it and the archetypal energies we summon start flowing through us more consistently. Ultimately, the creativity of Michelangelo is effortlessly flowing through you; Wonder Woman is riding shotgun; and Rosa Parks is sitting right next to you in the front seat of the bus.

These are just a few of my archetypes; but your life is unique and you have your own personal gods and goddesses sleeping inside. So let's awaken them by reflecting on this core question:

"What trait, skill set, or divine quality will I need to awaken from inside to shift my life from where it is to where I want it to be?"

Take a moment and let the answer bubble up. This requires honesty and your willingness to shine a bright light on all the shadowy areas of your life. Through honest reflection, you will be able to see what you need and what you don't have right now. This is where you get to awaken your sleeping god or goddess to help you: break out of being stuck, find your next gear, and step into your passion.

AWAKENING YOUR SACRED ARCHETYPES

When we *Awaken the Divine* to support us in taking our next step, then we are not leaping into the void by ourselves. We are fully empowered. This is how we move from simply having good intentions to full-on manifestation. Read the question below, and reply with your archetype.

Who is the archetype that you call on when you:

Need more strength? More courage? More grace? More compassion? More patience? More awareness? More resilience? More tenderness? More impeccability? More understanding? More determination? More creativity? More kindness? More forgiveness? More boldness? More wisdom? Who is the archetype you can call on to help you awaken the top three characteristics, core traits, skill sets, or strengths that will best move you through the challenge you wrote down when you were breaking through the clouds?

Your archetypes are flowing, so let's make your list of the top 10 traits you'd like to awaken and the archetype who embodies them. Write them down on the *My Sacred Archetypes* list, and read the list a few times throughout the day.

My Sacred Archetypes

	Trait	Archetype
1.		
2.		
3.		
4.		
5.		
6.		
7.		
8.		
9.		
10.		

This is the birthing part of the passion process that we have been cultivating all along. Feel free to delete archetypes that are no longer needed or who have worn out their usefulness and to add new ones as new challenges, circumstances, and situations reveal themselves. Keep your list in a place where you refer to it often and within a few days, you'll have them all at your fingertips. And whenever you need to reawaken your *Sacred Power of Passion*, call on your archetypes and watch your dreams and desires effortlessly translate into your reality.

THE SACRED FIRE OF YOUR MANIPURA

You must never forget that the sacred fire that burns within your manipura acts like a magnet to attract the limitless power of the Universe. The supernova outside of you and the radiant sun inside you are always connected, always communicating, always flowing energy back and forth. This means that even in your lowest moments, you are never stuck.

The Divine Principle of Inner Fire is an immutable law of the Universe that exists to remind you that in every moment, your flame can be reignited. The *Sacred Power of Passion* teaches that even in your darkest moment, your coolest ember is patiently resting deep within your manipura waiting for the Universe to reignite your flame. People can sit for years in pilot light mode, and then with a *whoosh!* re-engage their lives. This Sacred Power transcends all the excuses that your mind could ever conjure and flows through you in every moment.

THE SACRED QUESTIONS FOR AWAKENING PASSION

Before you go into silent meditation today and every day for the next week, identify a challenge in one of the five realms—physical, emotional, material, relationship, or spiritual—and call on the quality that would help you overcome it. Then call on an archetypal figure, person in your life (living or dead), mythical character, or "rock star" that resonates with you. And breathe that person into your awareness, inviting them into your very being. An easy way to spark this process is to silently ask yourself these questions:

"What does my heart long for?"

"What trait do I need?"

"Who can help me move from where I am to where I want to be?"

As you become more comfortable with this process, answers will consistently flow to you every day and you will feel your confidence and courage strengthen. The *Divine Principle of Inner Fire* is the core of your self-esteem. And when your manipura is shining brightly, you see beauty in yourself, in others, and all around you. You are so full of the fire of the universe that you radiate it effortlessly, stepping boldly into your power, and leaning hard in to your dreams. In this expanded state of clarity, self-confidence, and self-assurance, your *Sacred Power of Passion* will lead you to the ultimate fulfillment of your dreams.

CHAPTER TWENTY-EIGHT

THE SACRED POWER
OF PURPOSE

So, which is it? Let the Light decide, or never give up?
The answer is: both.

— Yehuda Berg

With an awakened heart and an activated passion, the *Divine Principle of Inner Fire* guides you to then answer your deepest question, "What is the meaning of my life?" Probably the most profound question you could ever ask, and the answer you arrive at, will propel you through life until you take your last breath. The ancient sages found the answers in the stars, and more specifically in a divine power, which they referred to in Sanskrit as *dhri* (pronounced dree). Literally translated as "to support, hold, or bear," *dhri* was the heavenly force that held the stars apart and the Universe together. *Dhri* was the cosmic energy that allowed everything to make sense, essentially the why and how of all existence.

The *Sacred Power of Purpose* is the law of nature that, once internalized, holds *your* stars apart and *your* Universe together. When you ask yourself what matters in life, the answers are the building blocks of your own personal *dhri*. The ancient Buddhists developed the word *dhamma* from the word *dhri* in order to describe the pure truth taught by the Buddha. To fully understand *dhri*, ask yourself right now, "What holds *my* stars apart and *my* Universe together?"

Some of us believe that we have been placed on this planet for a reason. The 12th-century Sufi poet Hafiz explained that our purpose is "to love more and be happy." The Bhagavad Gita explains that every being on the planet has been put here to fulfill a very specific purpose, and through our unique expression, we fulfill that cosmic aim. There are hundreds of ancient books, teachings, poems, and biblical references that elaborate on this idea of our role in the bigger picture. And regardless of your beliefs, you know you have a very personal *dhri*, something in your life that holds your stars apart and your universe together, something that is your most natural and unique expression, or simply the thing that makes you *you*!

Passion and purpose are cosmically interwoven: once you know what you most care about, you can start being more purposeful in the way that you think, speak, and act. So let's explore what you value, because these are the guardrails that you use to navigate yourself through the world. When you don't really know what matters, then you are aimless—careening back and forth between boundaries that are created by someone else or something other than you. When you truly know what you value, then your guardrails transform into nourishing guideposts that propel you further in the direction of your dream. The *Sacred Power of Passion* helps to keep you moving forward, but only when purpose is activated do you make more deliberate and conscious choices. In time, the laser focus of your manipura delivers you exactly to where you need to be to live your life with greater purpose.

WHAT MATTERS TO ME NOW?

The *Sacred Power of Purpose* is ever evolving as we move through the various phases of our life. What mattered to us in our youth may be very different from what mattered to us even five years ago. That's why this is an ongoing exploration, and as our life progresses, we will experience diverse expressions of our *dhri*.

You may be very clear on what you think matters to you right now. But how much of that is based on what's happened to you over the course of your life, and how you've reacted to it? On the other hand, how much of what matters to you in this moment is based on your divine purpose, or *dhri*? How much of who you are has been decided by your environment, your circumstances, and the people in your life versus that cosmic radiant light that shines from within and the pure expression of your native energies? Your life is a series of choices, and you've had to make some challenging and amazing decisions to get you this far. We know that at your core, you are pure, perfect, whole, and enlightened. But most likely, many of the decisions you've made came from scenarios in which you were forced to make a choice that ultimately was not in your best interest or not of your own design, and it did not support your divine purpose. Subsequently, the result pushed you off course in a direction away from your heart, passion, or your purpose.

The Path

So let's rediscover what really matters to you. The results will inspire you and help awaken your purpose! Take some quiet time, and grab a pen. These are some pretty direct questions, and the answers are meant to flow from the core of your being, not your intellect. Whenever you get stuck, place your hand on your heart, close your eyes, and just breathe for a minute as you move your attention from your head back into your heart. (Remember: the heart never lies!)

What Really Matters Worksheet

1. What are the five most defining moments I have had over the past three years (good and bad)? These are the moments where you made a choice or one was made for you that set you in a specific direction and started to define your thoughts, words, and actions.

    1. _____

    2. _____

    3. _____

    4. _____

    5. _____

---

2. What are the three most positive relationships I have intentionally entered into over the course of my life? And what three traits do I admire in each of those relationships?

Relationship   Trait 1   Trait 2   Trait 3

   1. _____

   2. _____

   3. _____

3. What are the three most important decisions I have made in my life that led to what I consider successes or accomplishments?

   1. _____

   2. _____

   3. _____

4. What are the three worst decisions I made in the last few years? (Choices that made me feel out of alignment or decisions that did not serve me or that I keep regretting.)

   1. _____

   2. _____

   3. _____

5. What are the three non-nourishing relationships in my life right now, and why have I chosen them?

Relationship   Reason for choosing

   1. _____

   2. _____

   3. _____

6. What are my top three time-wasting activities (activities that don't move you forward, support your vision, or align with your purpose)?

    1. _____

    2. _____

    3. _____

7. What three common themes are showing up in my life over the past 10 years and over the past year?

    Past 10 years

    1. _____

    2. _____

    3. _____

    This year

    1. _____

    2. _____

    3. _____

8. How do I define myself right now, in this moment? (Quickly list 10 ways you describe yourself.)

    1. _____

    2. _____

    3. _____

    4. _____

    5. _____

6. _____

7. _____

8. _____

9. _____

10._____

9. How do I want to define myself over the next 12 months?

_____

_____

_____

_____

_____

10. From the list below, circle the 10 values I hold most dear (the most defining principles that guide my words, actions, and choices).

Efficiency	Authenticity
Achievement	Available
Equality	Flexible
Purity	Open-hearted
Loyalty	Friendship
Belonging	Teamwork
Nurturing	Patience
Cleanliness	Perfection
Organized	Understanding
Gratitude	Diversity
Healthy	Accountability
Persistence	Fairness
Wealth	Kindness
Integrity	Fame
Encouraging	Reliability
Austerity	Merciful

Responsibility	Fitness
Order	Challenge
Goodness	Openness
Trust	Collaboration
Truth	Tradition
Discipline	Peace
Influence	Pleasure
Joy	Wisdom
Principled	Perseverance
Altruism	Defenselessness
Spirituality	Purposeful
Balance	Impact
Simplicity	Forgiving
Freedom	Status
Success	Generous
Passion	Authority
Happiness	Honesty
Creativity	Selfless
Humor	Bodhicitta
Power	Family
Elegance	Accurate
Adventure	Community
Fairness	Courage
Love	Inclusiveness

11. From your choices above, or any others you hold dear, list your seven most important values. These are your Seven Sacred Values.

1. _____
2. _____
3. _____
4. _____
5. _____
6. _____
7. _____

As you reflected on the answers to these questions, you've probably gone back in time to some challenging decisions. And if you proceeded thoughtfully, and took your time, you may even have learned something about yourself. The process may have sparked some emotion. This is good. Remember, we wanted to explore our choices from the level of the heart not the head. So now may be the time for tears, but it's definitely not the time for judgment! Now is the time to celebrate your courage for going into some scary, dark places on the journey to discover your soul.

A SINGLE FLAME

The intense process you just went through reveals several salient aspects of your life. It shows you clearly what you have cared about and the things that distinctly matter to you. But it may also have revealed the many distractions, roadblocks, and rabbit holes that led you away from your *dhri*. You may have been on track to achieve some very clear goals; but a choice here and a decision there, and suddenly you're on a very different path from the one you envisioned. And, most likely, in that critical moment, the flame burning brightly in your manipura went into pilot light mode.

Our world is overflowing with background noise, tempting interruptions, unexpected demands, and tantalizing possibilities. In every moment, there is one more thing to yank your attention away from what you truly care about. And when you look at your successes in life, they have all unfolded when you burned brightly in one clear direction with a single-mindedness of purpose. The moment a shiny object comes into your awareness to divert your attention from the mission, you need to be able to sidestep or repurpose it. The *Divine Principle of Inner Fire* teaches that the spark that lights your flame of purpose must come from a concentrated beam. That is why constantly using the filter of *nourishment or distraction* is so critical to staying on track and living each moment with purpose. As you begin to feel yourself moving away from your *dhri*, ask yourself, "Will this nourish my purpose? Or distract from it?" Always drift back to nourishment.

As you reflect on your Seven Sacred Values, there is probably one that is your guiding light, beating the loudest in your heart—one that allows you to say, "This is me!" Seize this value, build on it, say it out loud, weave it into your conversations, post it. We need to turn this inner conversation into your outer dialogue. And we can take powerful steps throughout the day to activate it and keep it alive as the target of your life. The *Sacred Power of Passion* drives our *dhri*, and we must keep asking, "What is the *one* thing that keeps my stars apart and holds my Universe together?"

MY SACRED VALUES

I live my life based on the Five Divine Principles contained in this book. Over the years, as I've gotten clearer on my native energies, who I am, and what truly matters to me, I've fine-tuned my own list of Sacred Values. I've changed my mind about a lot of things over the years, but I consider my Seven Sacred Values to be my pillars, the principles in my life that should come before anything else. And whenever I find myself confused, stuck, or conflicted on which direction I should turn, I go back to my list, remind myself what matters, and *live* the core value.

Living each day guided by the *Divine Principles of the Universe* is an evolutionary daily process, and it takes practice. One day at a time—one moment at a time—as we awaken our Sacred Powers, we learn to make our Sacred Values more important than anything else. They keep us on track, guide us to our true purpose, and help us make decisions that are aligned with our heart. For me, living them unfolded from my daily meditation practice. Then they began to enter my thoughts. Then they began trickling into my words. And only then did they begin to influence my behavior. Whenever I found myself out of integrity or challenged regarding how I was approaching a situation, I reflected on these values and lived the moment according to the light inside rather than what anyone else was expecting or demanding. I learned to say no a lot more, and I learned to really lean in to all those parts of my life where I was saying Yes.

Today, in this sacred, precious moment, as I write these words, I am clear on my seven Sacred Values. They are embedded in my heart. I have posted them on the wall of my office, taped to my bathroom mirror, and folded up inside my wallet. I don't share these out loud with other people, but every flicker of electricity that flows through my body simultaneously flows through these values before I am sparked to think, speak, or act. I share them here with you as a helpful tool to cultivating your own.

My seven Sacred Values:

Lead each moment with love. Others are suffering. Love them. Be grateful. Choose miracle over grievance in every moment. And root for others' suffering to end. Whatever the question, the answer is love.

Forgive and let go. Everyone deserves another chance. I deserve another chance. People who have hurt me deserve another chance. People who have tried but stumbled deserve another chance. Forgive and move on.

I am neither above nor below anyone. I am one with everything on the planet. We are all made up of that same stardust, which first birthed our world. Whatever I judge, reject, or embrace is simply a reflection of me.

Own my impact. No one else is determining how I feel or what I do. I take full responsibility and accountability for all my actions and their consequences, even when I did not anticipate them.

Authenticity. I am unique and not a version of anyone else. When I find my beliefs, words, or actions are out of alignment, I acknowledge it, own it, and rededicate myself to the best version of myself. Always flow my true essence, even if it humbles me and makes me appear smaller to others.

Service. The Universe is calling me in every moment to step up and make a difference. My *dhri* is to help, heal, and serve others. Each morning, I wake up, meditate, and then ask, "What will you have me do today?" and then listen to the whispers in the stillness of my heart.

Abundance. The Universe is infinite. There's enough love, money, happiness, and fulfillment for all of us in every moment. Whatever I need, I trust that I will receive it, especially when it doesn't appear obvious.

Just writing these right now has helped to strengthen my *dhri*. That's why I encourage you to go back to the seven Sacred Values you wrote down and spend some time with them over the next few days, weeks, and months until they ripple through you. Whenever I struggle with life, I come back to my Sacred Values, and ask, "Where have I drifted away from my balance?" "Where have I gone against what matters to me?" The answers flow and I evolve. I don't beat myself up for not living up to my standards; I celebrate the fact that I am aware of my drifting away and that I won't drift for one *more* moment. I rejoice in the knowledge that I am back on track.

These are just *my* Sacred Values. You have your own personal set, and perhaps you have not explored them until right now. But right now is the time to transform your concepts and thoughts into a tangible reality by moving them out of your head and into the real world onto a living, breathing document. As you continue to explore your Sacred Values, you may want to start with just one or two. In your final list, anywhere from three to seven will suffice, and that may shift over time as well. Even if it's not necessarily how you have been living it, ask yourself, "What is the way I want to live my life starting right now?"

With a broader understanding of what has mattered in your life and a deeper sense of what matters to you right now, the *Sacred Power of Purpose* will effortlessly guide your thoughts, your beliefs, your words, and your actions, into the fulfillment of your dream.

The *Divine Principle of Inner Fire* allows you to breathe in the Universe, harness its power, and direct that energy in three core areas of your life: the realms of your awakened heart, your passion, and your purpose. The resulting awakening of your Sacred Powers sparks a chain reaction, progressively expanding the ability of your heart to receive, then for your passion to be ignited, and, ultimately, for your purpose to crystallize. In this activated state, each Sacred Power flows individually. Then, as they start to interweave, a *symphonic* fusion occurs, culminating in a fiery crescendo of purposeful decision making.

CHAPTER TWENTY-NINE

LIVING THE DIVINE PRINCIPLE OF INNER FIRE

Don't only practice your art,
but force your way into its secrets.

— Ludwig van Beethoven

THE SACRED RITUALS FOR AWAKENING THE
DIVINE PRINCIPLE OF INNER FIRE

You can awaken the *Divine Principle of Inner Fire* in your life and the Sacred Powers of *Your Awakened Heart, Passion,* and *Purpose* through five powerful daily rituals that can be practiced individually or in combination. Each ritual offers you an opportunity to cultivate love, passion, purpose, and their magnificent fusion. All five practiced on a daily basis will transform you from the inside out:

Asking the Five Sacred Questions of Inner Fire

The Awakened Heart Meditation

The Sacred Affirmation of the Awakened Heart

The Inner Fire Sacred Mantra

The Sacred Rite for the Fire of Transformation

THE FIVE SACRED QUESTIONS OF INNER FIRE

We ask five Sacred Questions to expand your ability to open your heart more, spark your passion, and clarify your purpose:

1. Will I let love in today?
2. Who am I grateful for?
3. What does my heart long for?
4. What holds my stars apart and my Universe together?
5. What step can I take right now to help others and make a difference?

Simply ask each question over and over for about a minute. Sometimes answers will flow; sometimes there will be no answers. The key is to create an internal dialogue that over time becomes your external dialogue.

PRACTICING THE AWAKENED HEART MEDITATION

The Awakened Heart Meditation uses your heart as a starting point for gradually radiating loving-kindness outward into the world; and then expands your circle of loving-kindness. The practice uses your breath as a vehicle to channel *unconditional loving-kindness* (known in Sanskrit as *metta*) to heal your heart and *subsequently* heal the hearts of others.

First, place your hand on your heart and take a long, slow, deep breath in of unconditional loving-kindness. Feel it fill your heart, and slowly flow it back out as you exhale. Take another long, slow deep breath in of sweet metta and feel it fill your heart, and slowly flow it back out as you exhale. Slowly breathe it in; slowly let it go.

Now breathe in metta again even more deeply into your heart; feel it fill with love; and slowly flow it back out to those you deeply respect, such as your most revered teachers or life guides.

Next, take a long, slow, deep breath in of metta and feel it fill your heart, then as you exhale, radiate loving-kindness to your loved ones— those near, far, those living, and those who've left this earthly realm.

Again, take a long, slow deep breath in of metta and feel it fill your heart, and then as you exhale, radiate it out to all your friends—close and distant.

And now take a long, slow deep breath in of metta and feel it fill your heart, and, as you exhale, shower it onto someone you know who may be suffering, struggling, or in pain. Stay in this space for a few moments, breathing in healing love and flowing it back out to someone you know who's suffering.

By this time, your heart is overflowing with love—bursting with unconditional loving-kindness. You've got so much to give. You are simply a channel of love.

Next take a long, slow, deep breath in of metta and feel it fill your heart beyond its capacity, and then, as you exhale, radiate it out to someone with whom you have a grievance. Let that flow for a bit.

Now take a long, slow, deep breath in of metta and feel it fill your heart, and, as you exhale, radiate it out to all sentient beings on the planet. See your love showering the whole earth and everything on it.

Now take a long, slow, deep breath in of metta, feel it fill your heart, and then exhale, radiating that love out into the Universe, sending it to every corner of the galaxy.

Next breathe that metta in from every nook and cranny of the cosmos, feel it pour into your heart, and then radiate that infinite flow back into every cell in your body. Stay in this space for a few moments allowing the open-ness of your heart to flow love, gratitude, and self-compassion through every aspect of your being.

When it feels comfortable, take a long, slow, deep breath in and sigh as you exhale. Do that a few more times and you will feel how much lighter your heart is. A weight has been lifted. An open-ness has been created. Love is flowing.

Feel free to practice this with your eyes open or closed.

If you are experiencing any emotional constriction like holding a grudge, carrying around anger, feeling overwhelmed with sadness, or finding yourself pointing fingers of blame, the Awakened Heart Meditation will transform you to a healing state very quickly.

Take your time cultivating this heart practice. Start with just five minutes, get comfortable there, and then slow each phase of the process down until the conduit of your heart flows in and out in slow motion. Over time, see if you can stretch the meditation to 10, then 15 minutes—the perfect amount of time to receive the optimal benefits of a heart-opening practice. Visit davidji.com/SacredBonus to be guided through a gentle, expanded version of this practice.

After a few weeks of practicing this teaching, the Awakened Heart Meditation will become the gentle way you start your day. You'll quickly notice that you have washed away the barriers to love that once impeded you. You will realize that your heart is more open to kindness, compassion, and forgiveness; you are more tolerant of irritations around you; and you have the ripple of an awakened heart flowing through every word, thought, and action.

THE SACRED AFFIRMATION OF THE AWAKENED HEART

Repeat the *Sacred Affirmation* out loud five times; then whisper it five times; then repeat it silently to yourself for approximately one minute.

I am whole. I am loved. I am love. I am peace.

THE INNER FIRE SACRED MANTRA

The *Sacred Mantra* for awakening your inner fire is a transformational tool that can be woven into the very fiber of your being. These are the very first words of the Rig Veda, the oldest book known to man. They can be translated as "I surrender to the fire of transformation." Throughout the day, as you encounter change, confusion, upset, or surprise, close your eyes, take a long, slow, deep breath, and calmly repeat the mantra:

AGNI MEELE PUROHITAM
(ahg-nee mee-lay poor-oh hee-taam).

THE SACRED RITE FOR THE FIRE OF TRANSFORMATION

Stand or sit and stretch your hands as far as they will reach out to the sides. As you breathe in, slowly raise your heart up, and extend it forward as far as it will stretch. Out loud say, "Agni meele purohitam." Then whisper it one time. And then silently repeat it once. Then place your palms together and raise them to your heart, allowing your thumbs to rest against your heart center as you say out loud, "I surrender to the fire of transformation."

YOUR INNER FIRE IS ETERNAL

Each day that you practice the *Sacred Rituals of the Divine Principle of Inner Fire*, you will shift a bit toward clarity. Love will expand in your heart. Your passion will awaken in areas of your life you often dreamed about. And you will begin cultivating your purpose so that it ultimately becomes a powerful expression of your best version. Remember, as you grow and evolve, so will the many ways you express your heart, your passion, and your purpose. In time you will become masterful at balancing light and heat, and the choices you make in these core aspects of your BEing will continue to raise your vibration.

The Five Secrets, Divine Principles, and Sacred Powers

CHAPTER THIRTY

TAKING YOUR NEXT STEPS ON THE PATH

Ask and you shall receive; seek and you shall find; knock and the door shall be opened.

— Luke 11:9

THE FIRST SECRET: The Divine Principle of One
The Sacred Power of Presence
The Sacred Power of Your Ripple
The Sacred Power of Spirit

THE SECOND SECRET: The Divine Principle of Awareness
The Sacred Power of Attention
The Sacred Power of Intention
The Sacred Power of Action

THE THIRD SECRET: The Divine Principle of REbirth
The Sacred Power of Acceptance
The Sacred Power of Release
The Sacred Power of New Beginnings

THE FOURTH SECRET: The Divine Principle of Infinite Flow
The Sacred Power of Trust
The Sacred Power of Abundance
The Sacred Power of Shakti

THE FIFTH SECRET: The Divine Principle of Inner Fire
The Sacred Power of Your Awakened Heart
The Sacred Power of Passion
The Sacred Power of Purpose

If you've come this far with me, your life has already transformed and your personal evolution has firmly taken hold. Nature abhors a vacuum. Just by immersing yourself into this timeless wisdom, you are effortlessly exchanging so many of the old practices, habits, and perspectives you once held for new, life-affirming ones. Living a life filled with one-ness, awareness, REbirth, infinite flow, and inner fire is a gift you have given yourself.

Through the daily practice of awakening the Sacred Powers of Presence, Your Ripple, and Spirit in your life, you are living each moment in alignment with something much bigger than you—something sacred and divine. Through the daily practice of awakening the Sacred Powers of Attention, Intention, and Action, you have accelerated your ability to manifest your dreams, turning your good intentions into magnificent choices. Through the daily practice of awakening the Sacred Powers of Acceptance, Release, and New Beginnings, the baggage of your past no longer holds you back from stepping into your power. Through the daily practice of awakening the Sacred Powers of Trust, Abundance, and Shakti, you now flow the magnificent power of the Universe in moments where you once were fearful or played small. Through the daily practice of awakening the Sacred Powers of Your Awakened Heart, Passion, and Purpose, your sacred fire of transformation is burning brightly to guide you in the direction of love, satisfaction, and deeper fulfillment.

You are not alone on this journey. Every day thousands of people around the world are discovering the *Five Divine Principles* for the very first time. And thousands more are awakening their

Sacred Powers of Transformation to take their lives to the next level. I am grateful that you've taken the time to journey with me, and I'm honored that we have connected at such a deep level. I encourage you to connect with me at sacredpowers@davidji.com to share your story, your challenges, and your triumphs.

I've created a free online portal exclusively for you to connect more deeply with the teachings, listen to expanded guided meditations, and refresh your practice in those moments when constriction strikes or when you'd like a quick review. Join me at davidji.com/SacredBonus. In the meantime I encourage you to treat this book as a life guide, a real-world manual to help you step back into your power when you stumble, and a powerful tool to help you boldly soar to new heights as you raise the vibration of your best version.

I wrote this book with deep love in my heart, and I hope you have received it as we stepped together through the past and into the now. I send you my warmest wishes and my most healing intentions for a magnificent unfolding of the life of your dreams. Always remember the power of your ripple. Keep trusting, keep meditating, and keep awakening your Sacred Powers!

With love,
davidji

ACKNOWLEDGMENTS

So many people have been involved in the cultivation of my spiritual journey. And I am in awe of the love and support I've received from my friends, colleagues, students, and fellow teachers. Thank you for gracing me with your wisdom.

Profound gratitude to my teachers and friends Dr. Wayne Dyer, Dr. Deepak Chopra, Dr. David Simon, His Holiness the Dalai Lama, Barbara DeAngelis, Cheryl Richardson, don Miguel Ruiz, Mike Dooley, James Van Praagh, T. Harv Eker, Yogi Vishva, and the divine goddess of affirmations Louise Hay.

Special thanks to Reid Tracy for believing in me and trusting in my heart.

Thank you to my two life companions, my amazing wife, Rosanne, and my sweetheart Peaches, the Buddha Princess.

Gratitude to Michael Nila, Jack Hart, Dan Schmer, Howard Powers, and the devoted members of Blue Courage.

And to my relentless front row: Karla Refojo, Megan Monahan, Louise Pagmar, Suze Yalof, Laurent Potdevin, Michael Bloom, Tiffany Murray, Mindful Skater Girl, Ryananda Farquhar, Nicole Boxer, Abby Murphy, Diane Peterson, Krystal Wilson, Colleen Doumeng, Susan Francheschini, Robert and Linda Bray, Wanderlust, Grokker, lululemon, Nicole Richards, Amanda Ree and Rene Ringnalda, Gabrielle Forleo, Jennifer Templeton Clay, Leonie Gray Wolff, Diane Ray, Libby Carstensen, Richard Kwakernaak, Rosalinda Weel, Julia Anastasiou, Melissa Carver, Anna Dorwart, my Gottmer family, and the certified Masters of Wisdom and Meditation Teachers who ripple this timeless wisdom every day. I am in your front row!

Joyous appreciation to all those who have attended a davidji workshop, retreat, immersion, or training—you are my reason for waking up each day.

Thanks to my family of Jay and Charna, Stanley and Naomi, Susie and Jeffrey, Eddie and Kit.

Thank you to my Hay House family, who has rooted for me and supported my work every step of the way. My Hay House Radio family of Steve, Rocky, Mitch, Mike, and Rachel, who has kept LIVE! from the SweetSpot effortlessly flowing throughout the years.

None of my accomplishments would be possible without the devotion and tireless genius of my SweetSpot family of Somyr Perry, who swirls my heavens, Nancy MacLeod, who brings my heaven to earth, and Amelie Archer, who shines so brightly.

Eternal thanks to Patty Gift and Lisa Cheng for helping my book dreams become reality. And to Elisa Jordan for challenging my every keystroke.

Deep love to my dear Viking Queen Marianne Pagmar—the Love Shower—who lived every moment with such magnificent heart, profound grace, and unrivaled authenticity. I am better because you believed in me.

ABOUT THE AUTHOR

davidji is an internationally recognized pioneer in the teaching of *mindful performance*—essentially slowing down the world around you so you can make better choices in the moment, step into your power, and own your impact. He's developed signature heart-based techniques to help people move from mindless to mindful and each week, he shares these teachings on college campuses, with major league sports teams and high-pressured businesses, and with members of the military and law enforcement throughout the United States, Canada, Ireland, and the Netherlands.

davidji believes that we can transform the world around us by transforming ourselves. And he has pioneered his fusion of ancient wisdom, modern science, spirituality, and real-world practices to help people find their next gear, rediscover their purpose, and awaken to their best version.

After years of grinding it in the high-stress corporate world, he unplugged, left New York, and headed off on his own journey of personal transformation. He spent six months traveling through India in search of the Guru, where he realized that "the Guru rests inside" of us. He then apprenticed under Deepak Chopra for a decade as the Lead Educator and Dean of Chopra University, where he trained and certified over a thousand teachers in yoga, meditation, and Ayurveda.

davidji is credited with creating *the 21-day meditation* process and he has recorded more than 1,000 guided meditations to help people deepen their spiritual journey, cultivate their meditation practice, move beyond fear, eliminate anxiety, and step into their power. He is the author of the spiritual classic *Secrets of Meditation*, which won the Nautilus Book Award, and his critically acclaimed *destressifying* became an Amazon.com #1 bestseller. His meditation album *Fill What Is Empty; Empty What Is Full* has been downloaded and streamed over a million times.

davidji's *Masters of Wisdom & Meditation Teacher Training* encourages people to awaken the spiritual warrior resting inside and teaches timeless wisdom in a fresh, practical, and personal expression. You can join the SweetSpot Meditation Community at davidji.com.

davidji

transform the world *by transforming yourself*

visit davidji.com

For more information on meditation, conscious choice-making, stress management, heart healing, and integrating timeless wisdom into your daily life, visit www.davidji.com.

join the davidji sweetspot community

Sign up at davidji.com to be a member of the davidji sweetspot community, and receive regular tools, tips, and techniques to lessen stress, ease anxiety, and bring greater balance into your life including free meditations, stress busters, and ways to connect with the millions of meditators around the world.

follow davidji

 facebook.com/flowoflove

twitter.com/davidji_com

@davidjimeditation

Hay House Titles of Related Interest

YOU CAN HEAL YOUR LIFE, the movie,
starring Louise Hay & Friends
(available as an online streaming video)
www.hayhouse.com/louise-movie

THE SHIFT, the movie,
starring Dr. Wayne W. Dyer
(available as an online streaming video)
www.hayhouse.com/the-shift-movie

THE BIOLOGY OF BELIEF 10th ANNIVERSARY EDITION:
Unleashing the Power of Consciousness, Matter & Miracles,
by Bruce Lipton, Ph.D.

HEAL YOUR MIND: Your Prescription for Wholeness
through Medicine, Affirmations, and Intuition,
by Mona Lisa Schulz, M.D., Ph.D., with Louise Hay

HUMAN BY DESIGN: From Evolution by Chance
to Transformation by Choice, by Gregg Braden

THE MINDBODY SELF: How Longevity Is Culturally Learned
and the Causes of Health Are Inherited, by Dr. Mario Martinez

All of the above are available at your local bookstore,
or may be ordered by contacting Hay House (see next page).

We hope you enjoyed this Hay House book. If you'd like to receive our online catalog featuring additional information on Hay House books and products, or if you'd like to find out more about the Hay Foundation, please contact:

Hay House, Inc., P.O. Box 5100, Carlsbad, CA 92018-5100
(760) 431-7695 or (800) 654-5126
(760) 431-6948 (fax) or (800) 650-5115 (fax)
www.hayhouse.com® • www.hayfoundation.org

———

Published in Australia by: Hay House Australia Pty. Ltd.,
18/36 Ralph St., Alexandria NSW 2015
Phone: 612-9669-4299 • *Fax:* 612-9669-4144
www.hayhouse.com.au

Published in the United Kingdom by: Hay House UK, Ltd.,
The Sixth Floor, Watson House, 54 Baker Street, London W1U 7BU
Phone: +44 (0)20 3927 7290 • *Fax:* +44 (0)20 3927 7291
www.hayhouse.co.uk

Published in India by: Hay House Publishers India,
Muskaan Complex, Plot No. 3, B-2, Vasant Kunj, New Delhi 110 070
Phone: 91-11-4176-1620 • *Fax:* 91-11-4176-1630
www.hayhouse.co.in

———

Access New Knowledge.
Anytime. Anywhere.

Learn and evolve at your own pace
with the world's leading experts.

www.hayhouseU.com